COACH'S MANUAL

POWERZONE SPORTS CAMP

Heart of a WINNER

A COMPLETE GUIDE TO ORGANIZING A FIVE-DAY SPORTS CAMP
THAT COMBINES ATHLETIC AND SPIRITUAL TRAINING

FELLOWSHIP OF
CHRISTIAN ATHLETES

Gospel Light

HOW TO MAKE CLEAN COPIES FROM THIS BOOK

You may make copies of portions of this book with a clean conscience if

• you (or someone in your organization) are the original purchaser;

• you are using the copies you make for a noncommercial purpose (such as teaching or promoting your ministry) within your church or organization;

• you follow the instructions provided in this book.

However, it is ILLEGAL for you to make copies if

• you are using the material to promote, advertise or sell a product or service other than for ministry fund-raising;

• you are using the material in or on a product for sale; or

• you or your organization are not the original purchaser of this book.

By following these guidelines you help us keep our products affordable.

Thank you,

Gospel Light

Scripture quotations are taken from the *Holy Bible, New International Version®*. Copyright © 1973, 1978, 1984 by International Bible Society. Used by permission of Zondervan Publishing House. All rights reserved.

Many thanks to Karen Hughes and Christy Weir for helping to develop this material.

This edition issued by special arrangement with Fellowship of Christian Athletes, 8701 Leeds Rd., Kansas City, MO 64129, www.fca.org.

Original title: *Power Camp*

Contents

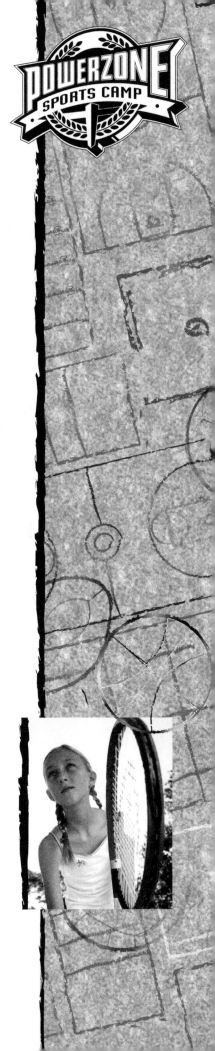

PRE-CAMP 5

CAMP PROGRAM 59

POST-CAMP 97

FIELD DIAGRAMS 103

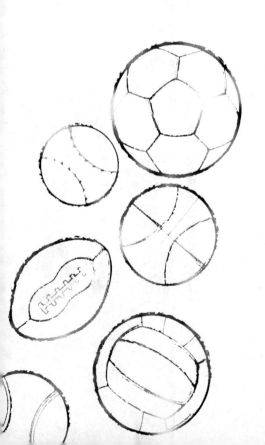

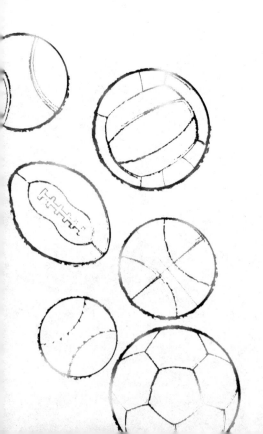

PowerZone Introduction

The PowerZone Manual that you are holding in your hands is a great ministry tool to reach your community for Christ through sports. PowerZone is a youth sports camp designed for young athletes from the ages of 8 to 12 who want to develop their athletic skills. PowerZone is an incredible day camp experience for any young athlete. Each day includes solid physical and spiritual training from coaches and athletes, as well as dynamic speakers, Bible studies and much, much more.

The goal is to reach young athletes and provide them with instruction and competition through a sport–specific and multi-sport focus. PowerZone is normally a summer day camp that involves the local community and church; however, it also can be done as an overnight camp experience, a weekend retreat, on five consecutive Saturdays, or during school breaks any time of the year.

This Manual will help you structure your PowerZone and organize the Practices, Huddles, Power Boosts and more. Please utilize these great resources and make a point to integrate them into your camp experience. The PowerZone program has a very intentional daily flow for campers and coaches to experience throughout the camp. From the devotionals to team meetings to huddles, they all focus on and develop the camp theme "Heart of a Winner."

PowerZone provides an exciting atmosphere where the entire community can see the impact of sports ministry in action. There is usually low overhead cost, which allows your church to offer the camp experience for a reasonable fee and increase the potential of generating revenue for your ministry. God will use your Power-Zone to reach athletes.

PowerZone Philosophy

What Is PowerZone?

PowerZone is an incredible experience for any young athlete. Each day includes solid athletic training, Bible studies, fun games and much, much more. This is an incredible opportunity to impact the young athletes and families of your area.

PowerZone is an opportunity to involve the children's and youth ministries of your church and other churches, and high school, college and professional athletes and coaches. PowerZone provides an exciting atmosphere where the entire community can experience ministry in action.

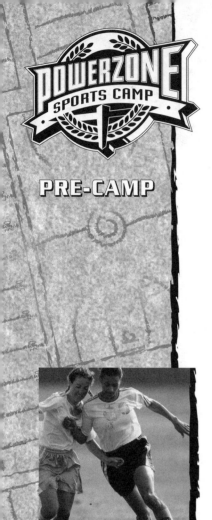

Key Power Verses

Here are three key verses that express what God can do with PowerZone:

▼ "I raised you up for this very purpose, that I might display my power in you and that my name might be proclaimed in all the earth." Romans 9:17

▼ "For the message of the cross is foolishness to those who are perishing, but to us who are being saved it is the power of God." 1 Corinthians 1:18

▼ "For God did not give us a spirit of timidity, but a spirit of power, of love and of self discipline." 2 Timothy 1:7

PowerZone Basics

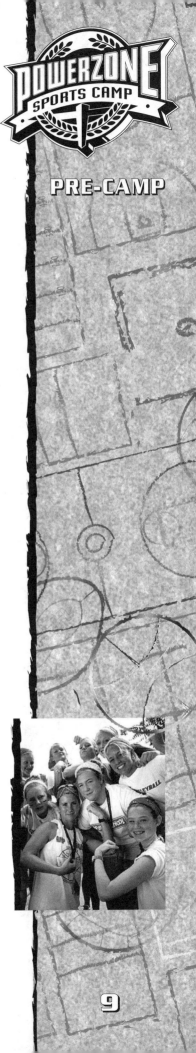

Here are the PowerZone Basics that will help you understand the big picture.

▼ PowerZone Sports Camps are usually local summer day camps, but can be scheduled at other times (weekend retreats, five consecutive Saturdays, school breaks any time of year).

▼ The strategy is to reach 8 to 12 year olds.

▼ The schedule of the day is 8:30 A.M.—4:00 P.M.

▼ PowerZone is usually sport-specific, so campers pick one sport to develop for the week.

▼ You can offer just one sport or over 10. Know your local community and the sports needs.

▼ The camp attendance can be 25 to 500 campers.

▼ Campers bring their lunch—you provide drinks and a snack each day.

▼ Your church can offer a quality sports camp for 8 to 12 year olds for a fraction of the cost of a regular sports camp.

▼ PowerZone is an opportunity to recruit volunteer coaches and athletes: high school coaches, local coaches/parents, high school students, youth pastors. Many volunteers cannot go away to a camp for the week, but they can plug into the PowerZone by helping several hours a day or just one full day.

▼ There are no traveling expenses and no meal expenses!

▼ Raise sponsorship or underwriting from local businesses (banners, logos on T-shirts, snacks, etc.).

▼ With only two practices a day, it is easy to get assistant coaches to help.

▼ PowerZone opens a whole new ministry opportunity for coaches who can't go away to overnight camp.

▼ Utilize local students as Huddle Leaders. Huddle Leaders must be 16 years and older. Students 15 and younger can be Junior Huddle Leaders (assistant leaders).

▼ PowerZone can be held at your church, at one of your local public middle or high schools, or at city or county parks and recreational facilities. Christian schools can also be a great location if they have the needed facilities and fields.

▼ Involve other churches in your community. They are always looking for new things to do for their 8 to 12 year olds—something other than VBS!

▼ Local youth pastors can serve as: Team Chaplain, Worship Leader, Guest Speaker, etc.

▼ Parents love PowerZone! Parents can volunteer as: assistant directors, meal director, medical staff, coaches, speakers, sponsors.

▼ Friday is Parents' Day and it gets the whole family involved.

▼ Determine the registration fee for PowerZone based on the quality of athletic instructors, facility rental costs and typical sports camp rates in your community. PowerZone has the potential to produce revenue.

THE BIBLICAL FOUNDATIONS

The following fundamentals address all aspects of the program and must be the guide for the camp staff as they deliver the camp message.

Share Jesus

Man originally had a relationship with God and was created in His image (Genesis 1:26). However, the devastation of the Fall has had dramatic effects in every area of the creation (Genesis 3:14-19). As a result, at camp we share that it is Jesus who restores our relationship with God (John 14:6). Sharing Jesus must not be limited to the Warm-Up assemblies, but rather it must naturally flow into the athletic training, competitions, Huddle times, etc. It is important that the Team Chaplain, who will deliver the Camp Theme, be selected from individuals who are employed in the church.

Seek Jesus

When we as broken and sinful beings come to Jesus, we are made new (2 Corinthians 5:17). Through this personal relationship we have an opportunity to grow in our love for Him (Revelations 2:4-5) and to be transformed (Romans 12:2). This should be done through specific camp activities such as prayer (Ephesians 6:18), studying the Word (Hebrews 4:12; Colossians 3:16) and worship (John 2:24; Hebrews 10:1). However, everything at camp should assist the campers in seeking Jesus, whether they are in the middle of competition or in a Huddle. When they leave, campers should be equipped with the skills that are necessary in actively seeking Christ.

Lead Others

Strong leaders who have strong leadership skills are critical to our camps. All leaders at PowerZone must first realize that the beginning of leadership is the fear and respect of God (Proverbs 19:23) and that leaders must reflect Jesus in all areas of their life (Proverbs 20:7; 1 Thessalonians 4:11).

Love Others

PowerZone is the perfect place for people to see and feel the love of Christ (Matthew 22:37-39; John 13:35; Philippians 2:1-5). God designed us to dwell together in a harmonious environment. The time spent in such an intense, godly setting results in campers experiencing Jesus' love in a significant way.

PowerZone Pack

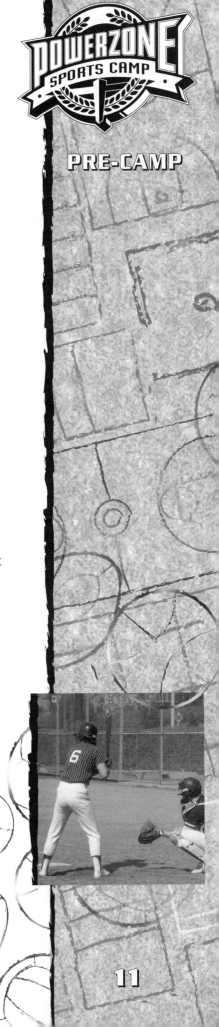

Your PowerZone Pack contains everything you need to promote and conduct an effective sports camp.

Each Pack Includes the Following:

▼ *PowerZone Coach's Manual* with organizing, recruiting and publicity materials; Bible theme studies; small group activities; and forms. Includes a CD-ROM that contains all the material in the manual.

▼ *The Heart of a Coach*, which is a daily devotional from Fellowship of Christian Athletes.

▼ *Coach Wooden's Pyramid of Success Playbook* by John Wooden and Jay Carty, who give practical, down-to-earth, biblical tips for being successful in life.

A Sample of Each of the Following:

▼ T-shirt that can be used to identify staff or to give every camper a personal sports-camp memento.

▼ Iron-on transfer for creating your own sports camp T-shirts.

▼ A Cap that can be given to Coaches and/or Huddle Leaders.

▼ H.E.A.R.T. wristbands that help kids remember what it means to have the Heart of a Winner.

▼ Four sports cones for Coaches to use on the playing field.

▼ Water bottles are a must-have for all your staff and campers.

▼ Whistles and lanyards for Coaches to use on the playing field.

PowerZone Logos

These logos are designed specifically for PowerZone. Using a logo designed specifically for your camp sets your camp apart. Using the PowerZone logo helps to better inform those whom you are trying to reach. Use the logo everywhere.

On the CD-ROM included in this book, you will find logos in the following formats:

TIFF — This format is great for your in-office printing and design.

JPEG — This format is great for use on your website.

EPS — This format is used by professional printers.

Checklist

The following is a checklist that will help you get your PowerZone off to a great start. Each of these are vital to making sure you have a great PowerZone. Be sure that each are completed before your camp begins:

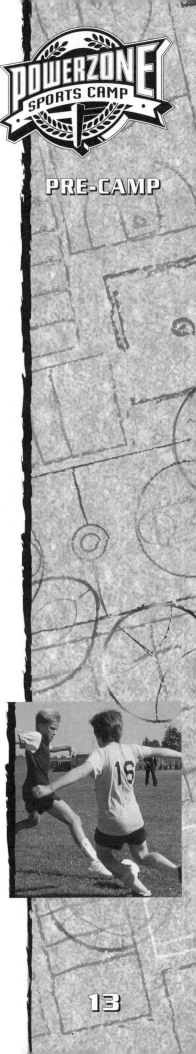

Six Months Prior

▼ Prayerfully decide to do a PowerZone.

▼ Begin to pray for and think about coaches and a location: What sports will you do? What equipment will be needed?

▼ Develop a budget.

▼ Determine Scholarship Amounts.

Five Months Prior

▼ Begin putting together Huddle Leader Notebooks with pertinent Information (see Pre-Camp Training).

▼ Select and Secure Site, Dates, Sports and Details.

▼ Recruit Core Staff: Director, Asst. Director, Huddle Leader Coordinator, Registrar.

▼ Prepare mailings to recruit Head Coaches and Huddle Leaders.

▼ Project camp size and number of Huddle Leaders and volunteers needed.

▼ Create Registration Form.

▼ Set daily Schedule and Program.

Four Months Prior

▼ Meet with Registrar about the registration process: Registration Forms, Enrollment Confirmation packet, etc.

▼ Publicize PowerZone: Parent mailings, local sport leagues, etc.

▼ Confirm Coaches (and their children).

▼ Create publicity pieces and publicize PowerZone: Posters, radio ads, church bulletin inserts, public service announcements, etc.

▼ Create Enrollment Confirmation packet: Enrollment Confirmation Form, Permission Waiver Form, Medical Release Form and Pick-up Form.

▼ Begin recruiting speakers, sponsors, Huddle Leaders, staff, etc.

▼ Set a Preregistration deadline for campers to receive an early registration discount. Make it worth registering early—even $25 cheaper! (This greatly helps with planning numbers.)

Three Months Prior

▼ Give poster and registration forms to everyone you know who would be interested in helping and ask them to help put up the posters and hand out brochures at local businesses, churches, event centers, etc.

▼ Confirm Huddle Leaders and Coaches.

▼ Continue Recruiting Staff: Worship Leader, Chaplain, Pro-File Speakers, Medical Staff, Water/Snack Team, Recreation Director.

▼ Work on obtaining sponsors.

▼ Confirm Equipment needed.

Two Months Prior

▼ Publicize at church events.

▼ Continue confirming camp details.

▼ Try to get snacks/drinks for campers and/or food for Huddle Leaders and Coaches donated for camp. Participating local businesses can get their logo on the PowerZone T-shirt.

▼ Finalize site, coaches, Huddle Leaders, volunteers, set-up needs.

▼ Publicize cut-off date for cheaper price.

One Month Prior

▼ Make sure registration confirmations are being sent out.

▼ Make one final push on early registration deadline; encourage early registration!

▼ Choose and train PowerBoy/Girl.

▼ Purchase drinks, snacks, first aid, Recreation time needs, etc.

▼ Confirm field and gym usage, fields mowed, equipment needed, etc.

▼ Confirm and train Huddle Leaders and Coaches. Have at least two training times and group prayer time for camp. Go over schedule, details, roles, etc. (See Pre-Camp Training.)

▼ Inventory deliveries, etc.

After PowerZone

▼ Send follow-up camp letter to all campers (include next year's dates).

▼ Send thank-you letters to everybody who served, donated, etc.

▼ Try to return lost and found items.

▼ Follow up with campers who made first-time decisions for Christ.

Setting Date and Securing Site

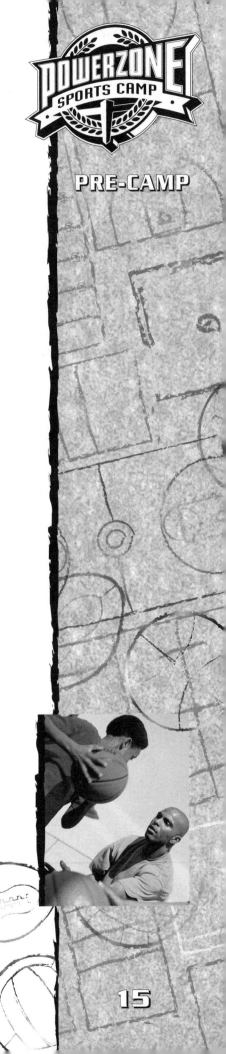

Setting Date

Anytime (summer, school breaks, weekend retreats, or five consecutive Saturdays) is a good time for a PowerZone. If you are planning a summer camp, the best time to offer the camp is the week following school dismissal. County programs held in the schools usually have not begun, as well as family vacations. Be sure to check with major churches in the area so that they may schedule their summer programs around your camp, as well as promote your camp. This is a great partnership opportunity!

Securing Site

If you do not have adequate athletic facilities at your church, contact schools, city recreation departments, county parks or private clubs in your community. Christian schools, as well as other churches, will often donate the use of their facility.

Key Staff Positions

Be sure to use the members of your church and community.

Camp Director

Pre-Camp

The role of Camp Director prior to camp is to serve as the administrator and meeting planner for site logistics, staffing, programming and scheduling.

On-Site

The role of the Camp Director during camp is to serve as coach, mentor and servant. The Director should fine-tune, refine, encourage, assist and inspire the staff.

Post-Camp

Hold a Post-Camp debriefing with Camp Staff and key site personnel on the last day of camp. Conduct facilities review with site representative and Assistant Director, including facility damage report. The Director must be the last staff person to leave the site—after all supplies and equipment have been cleaned up and paperwork has been completed. No camper should be left on-site unsupervised.

Assistant Director

The Assistant Director reports to the Camp Director. The Assistant Director helps the Camp Director in staffing, administration and program needs relating to Pre-Camp, On-Site and Post-Camp. The Assistant Director is to be the Director's arms and legs throughout the week—meeting site personnel, helping with program and administrative needs. You will be on call to the Camp Director, Site Contact and Medical Staff. In case of an accident or injury, you may be needed to take an individual to the doctor or hospital. You will verify receipts after registration is completed with Registrar. Conduct the Post-Camp Damage Report with the Site Contact, then review Report with Camp Director. Assist Director in conducting Post-Camp debriefing and evaluation session with Staff.

Huddle Leader Coordinator

The primary responsibility of the Huddle Leader Coordinator is to recruit, train and develop effective Huddle Leaders at camp. Plan to meet with all Huddle Leaders prior to camp to give instruction on Bible Study materials and to give Huddle Leader responsibilities during the Daily Schedule. The Huddle Leader Coordinator leads a daily devotional and prayer time before camp begins each day and leads a time at the end of each day to meet with Huddle Leaders to evaluate that day of camp and to notify Huddle Leaders of any upcoming information for the following days.

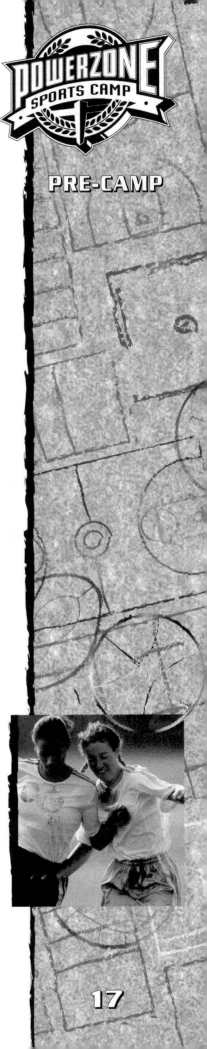

Registrar

The Registrar is responsible for the registration of each camper. The Registrar must be sure that each camper is accounted for daily and has completed payment, Permission Form and Pick-Up Form. Registrar is at camp each day to check-in campers and to make sure that each camper is picked-up by the person indicated on his or her Pick-Up Form.

Idea

After first day of camp, compile lists of campers in each Huddle. Give the lists of campers to each Huddle Leader to check off their campers as they arrive at camp each day. Ask Huddle Leaders to turn in their lists to you at the first meeting. Read off names of any campers who have not been accounted for. When campers hear their names, they are to stand and yell the camp Theme with great enthusiasm. This is fun, plus it is a good way to account for late arriving campers.

Power Boy/Girl

A great addition to any camp! Every camp needs mystery, excitement and a superhero. Power Boy or Girl may appear any time during the day to lead campers in exercises or songs, and/or to give information about activities and the schedule. The individual serving as Power Boy or Girl must never reveal his or her identity but may sign autographs at the end of camp. This is great fun for campers, especially for the younger athletes.

Team Chaplain

(Great place to use your youth minister.)

The Team Chaplain's role at camp is to help the campers understand the day's theme and encourage the campers to focus on the theme throughout the day. The Team Chaplain shares at the beginning of each day during the Warm-Up assembly.

Recreation Director

(Great place to use a physical education teacher or a youth minister.)

The Recreation Director is responsible for Recreation time. This is the time of camp when all or a majority of the campers are together to play. It may look a great deal like organized chaos. Have the Recreation Director organize games for all to participate in, such as relay races, tag games, etc. Make use of Huddle Leaders and other staff to help direct campers during this time.

Water/Lunch/Snack Person

This is a vital position for the success of camp. Water must be on the fields and available at every court before every practice begins. Have one person or a team of people specifically designated for this task. This person or team of people is also responsible for making sure that the drinks are cold for lunch and snack time. This person or team of people is also responsible for regulating the distribution of drinks and snacks at LUNCH and SNACK time.

Medical Staff

(Great place to use local high school or college trainer.)

Medical Staff is essential. A nurse and/or trainer must be on-site for any emergencies. All staff and campers should know where to find the Medical Staff at all times. Place them in a designated area for the entire camp. The Medical Staff, Camp Director, Assistant Director and Huddle Leader Coordinator should all know the location and quickest route to the nearest hospital.

Huddle Leaders*

(Great place to use high school and college athletes.)

The Huddle Leaders are some of the most important Staff at camp. Good Huddle Leaders will make your camp a huge success. Recruit them early and train them well. Target college and high school students who are willing to serve and who will relate well to your target age group. The Huddle Leaders are responsible for their designated group of campers all week long. Huddle Leaders must know where each of their campers is at all times.

*Huddle Leaders must complete the Ministry Leader Application and attend the Pre-Camp Training Session.

Coaching Staff*

(Great place to use local high school, college and professional coaches and athletes.)

The Head Coach of each sport is responsible for the Practice sessions. Each Head Coach may want to assemble his or her own coaching staff to assist in running each Practice, but Huddle Leaders are available to assist each Coach. Practice should consist of skill training and opportunities for competition. The Coaches should also be aware of the day's theme so that they may emphasize the theme during Practice. The Head Coach introduces and leads (with assistance from Huddle Leaders) the daily Power Boost devotional time.

*Be sure that each Coach has completed the Ministry Leader Application.

Worship Leader

(Great place to use your youth or children's minister or your church's worship band.)

The Worship Leader is responsible for leading singing during the Pro-File assemblies. Be sure that the Worship Leader will lead songs and have a personality that will relate well to your target age group.

Pro-File Speaker(s)

(Great place for local professional or college athletes or coaches to travel a short distance to serve for a short amount of time.)

These individuals should be able to share about their sport and their faith. They should be able to share in such a way that they relate well to the age group that is in attendance at your camp. It is important to have speakers that are representative of all the sports offered at your camp. Campers and parents are also appreciative when the athletes can stay after speaking to sign autographs.

Idea

Have your Pro-File Speaker be unannounced each day. This creates excitement!

Idea

Have trading cards, magazines or other items that you can give the campers to take home and remember what they have heard.

Idea

Have the Pro-File Speaker located past the camper Pick-Up point so that Pick-Up point does not get too congested.

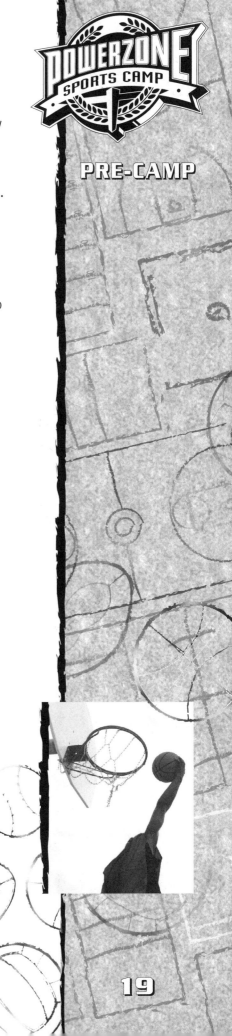

Posters

Posters are a must! This is a great way to create excitement about your camp.

Placement: Be sure to put posters everywhere, especially in churches, in youth and children's departments, in grocery stores, schools, and youth centers.

The following posters are samples of the types of posters that you can create. Be sure to note all of the important information on the sample poster. The posters are designed for printing on 8½" x 11" paper. The following posters offer two options. One is to write or paste your information directly on the poster. Second, you may want a professional printer to put your information directly on the poster. On the CD-ROM included in this book, you will find posters (both color and black and white) in the following formats:

TIFF — This format is great for your in-office printing and design.

JPEG — This format is great for use on your website.

EPS — This format is used by professional printers.

If you only need to print a few of these, place the TIFF image on a new document in Word. Add your local information and then print.

POWERZONE SPORTS CAMP

PowerZone 2006 is an incredible Day Camp experience for any 8- to 12-year-old athlete.

Each day includes SOLID athletic training from coaches and athletes, as well as DYNAMIC athlete speakers, BIBLE studies and much, much more.

HEART OF A WINNER

Thomas Jefferson High School

1234 North Street, Anytown, USA

$150*

***if registered before June 1, or $175 after**

To register, call
555-555-1212

(Date)

PowerZone 2006 is an incredible Day Camp experience for any 8- to 12-year-old athlete.

Each day includes SOLID athletic training from coaches and athletes, as well as DYNAMIC athlete speakers, BIBLE studies and much, much more.

HEART OF A WINNER

(Location)

(Phone Number)

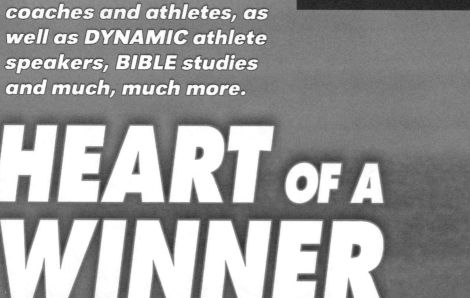

Letterhead

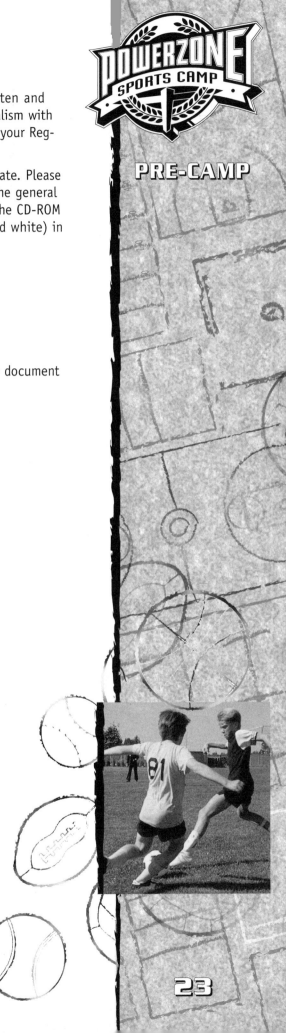

Letterhead is a wonderful thing to have. All camp correspondence written and typed should be on your letterhead. It creates excitement and professionalism with your camp. Especially use Letterhead to write the letter that will go with your Registration Form.

The following Letterhead is a sample of the Letterhead that you can create. Please note the important information at the bottom of the Letterhead. Use the general Letterhead to create your own personal Letterhead for your camp. On the CD-ROM included in this book, you will find Letterhead (both color and black and white) in the following formats:

TIFF — This format is great for your in-office printing and design.

JPEG — This format is great for use on your website.

EPS — This format is used by professional printers.

If you only need to print a few of these, place the TIFF image on a new document in Word. Then add your local information and print.

(address) ▼ (phone number) ▼ (e-mail address) ▼ (website)

Registration Form

Registration Forms are important tools for getting participants for PowerZone. Registration Forms should be easy to read and contain essential information about the camp that is being offered—date, time, location, price, who the camp is targeting, and who to contact for the camp. It is best if the Registration Form is easily reproducible and inexpensive. Be sure that your Registration Forms get into the right hands—local ministry databases, youth centers, youth leagues, churches, children's ministries, coaches, etc.

The following Registration Forms may be printed from your office computer. When you create your camp's Registration Form, be sure to include all of the important information shown on the sample. On the CD-ROM included in this manual, you will find Registration Forms (both color and black and white) in the following formats:

TIFF — This format is great for your in-office printing and design.

JPEG — This format is great for use on your website.

EPS — This format is used by professional printers.

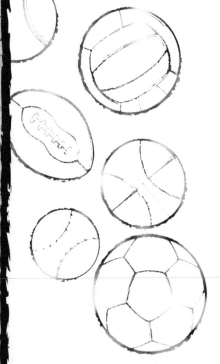

POWERZONE WILL BE HELD AT

Thomas Jefferson High School

1234 North Street, Anytown, USA

ON THE FOLLOWING DATES

June 20-June 24 Monday-Friday, 8:30 AM-4:00 PM

TO REGISTER, CALL

555-555-1212

PowerZone 2006 is an incredible Day Camp experience for any 8- to 12-year-old athlete. Each day includes SOLID athletic training from coaches and athletes, as well as DYNAMIC athlete speakers, BIBLE studies and much, much more.

Camper's Name _____   Church Name _____

Parent's Name _____   Parent's Signature _____

Sex ❑ M   ❑ F   Age _____   Adult T-Shirt Size _____   Height _____   Weight _____

Address _____

City _____   State _____   Zip _____

Credit Card number ❑ Visa   ❑ MC   ❑ Discover   Name on Card _____

Evening Phone number _____   Day Phone number _____   E-mail _____

Sport that you want to specialize in

❑ Baseball   ❑ Basketball   ❑ Football   ❑ Lacrosse   ❑ Soccer   ❑ Softball   ❑ Tennis   ❑ Volleyball

$150 per Camper, if registered before June 1, 2006. $175 after June 1 (check or credit card)

Return form to _____
(church address, phone, fax and e-mail)

POWERZONE WILL BE HELD AT

ON THE FOLLOWING DATES

TO REGISTER, CALL

PowerZone 2006 is an incredible Day Camp experience for any 8- to 12-year-old athlete. Each day includes SOLID athletic training from coaches and athletes, as well as DYNAMIC athlete speakers, BIBLE studies and much, much more.

Camper's Name _____   Church Name _____

Parent's Name _____   Parent's Signature _____

Sex ❑ M ❑ F   Age _____   Adult T-Shirt Size _____   Height _____   Weight _____

Address _____

City _____   State _____   Zip _____

Credit Card number ❑ Visa   ❑ MC   ❑ Discover   Name on Card _____

Evening Phone number _____   Day Phone number _____   E-mail _____

Sport that you want to specialize in

❑ Baseball   ❑ Basketball   ❑ Football   ❑ Lacrosse   ❑ Soccer   ❑ Softball   ❑ Tennis   ❑ Volleyball

$150 per Camper, if registered before June 1, 2006. $175 after June 1 (check or credit card)

Return form to _____

(church address, phone, fax and e-mail)

Medical Release Form

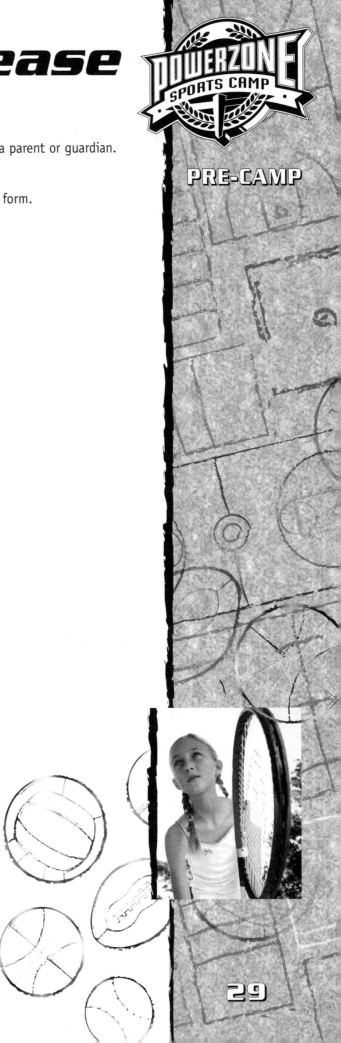

Each camper must turn in a Medical Release Form completed by a parent or guardian.

On the CD-ROM included in this manual, you will find a sample form.

Medical Release Form

POWERZONE SPORTS CAMP

(Church Name) _____

(Address) _____

(Phone Number) _____

Child's Name _____

Birth Date _____ Grade _____

Address _____

City, State _____ Zip _____

Phone Number _____

Date(s) of Activity _____

Authorization of Consent for Treatment of Minor

I, the undersigned parent or guardian of _____ ,
a minor, do hereby authorize any duly authorized employee, volunteer or other representative of (church
name) as agent(s) for the undersigned, to consent to any X-ray examination, anesthetic, medical or surgical
diagnosis or treatment, and hospital care which is deemed advisable by, and is to be rendered under the
general or specific supervision of, any licensed physician, dentist or surgeon, whether such diagnosis or
treatment is rendered at the office of said physician, dentist or surgeon or at a clinic, hospital or other
medical facility.

It is understood that this authorization is given in advance of any specific diagnosis, treatment or hospital
care being required, but is given to provide authority and power on the part of our aforesaid agent(s) to
give specific consent to any and all such diagnosis, treatment or hospital care which the aforementioned
physician, dentist or surgeon in the exercise of his or her best judgment may deem advisable.

This authorization shall remain effective from _____ to _____ .

Signature _____

Recruiting Coaches

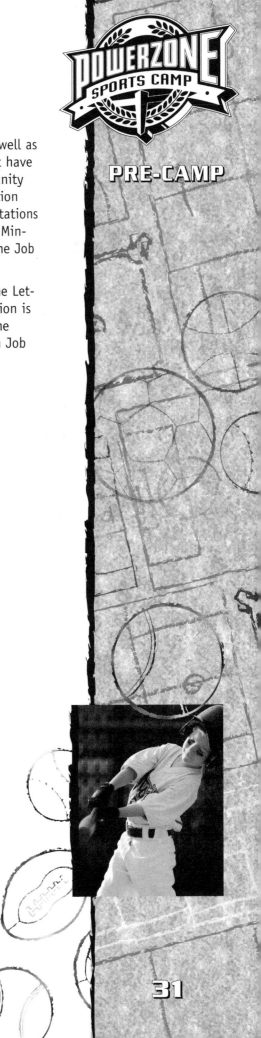

PowerZone is an incredible way to plug in local High School Coaches, as well as area Professional Athletes and Coaches. The benefits are that they do not have to travel very far, they may go home at night, and they have the opportunity to give back to their community. The following Power Coach Job Description gives the Coaches that you are recruiting their responsibilities and expectations for the week. It is extremely important that every Power Coach fill out a Ministry Leader Application. As you recruit coaches you need to send both the Job Description and the Ministry Leader Application to each potential coach.

The following pages include a sample letter to your Coaches on PowerZone Letterhead and a Power Coach Job Description. The Ministry Leader Application is on page 52. On the CD-ROM included in this manual, you will also find the sample letter to your Coaches on PowerZone Letterhead, the Power Coach Job Description and the Ministry Leader Application.

Dear Coach,

(Name of Church) is excited to announce PowerZone 2006. PowerZone is for 8- to 12-year-old boys and girls surging through this area (dates). I would like to extend to you the exciting opportunity of applying to be a POWER COACH at PowerZone 2006. Each POWER day will begin at 8:00 AM and will end at 4:30 PM. We already have some of the area's top high school coaches, collegiate and high school athletes scheduled for this week. A surprise athlete will also attend our PRO-FILE time to share about his or her faith each day. Below is the POWER SCHEDULE for each day.

You have been given this invitation because we believe that you could be a vital part of the PowerZone Team in reaching others for Christ. You have been asked to apply for the POWER COACH position because of your leadership ability and your desire to serve God and reach others.

Please look closely at the enclosed materials and prayerfully determine if this is where God would have you serve. If you discover that this is where God would have you serve, complete the Ministry Leader Application and return it to me by (date). If you have any questions, please do not hesitate to contact me. We are looking forward to serving with you at PowerZone!

POWER SCHEDULE	
8:30	Warm-Up
9:00	Power Boost
9:15	Practice
10:45	Huddle
11:30	Lunch
12:00	Recreation
12:45	Huddle
1:15	Practice
2:45	Snack
3:15	Pro-File
4:00	Pick 'em Up

(Your Name)
PowerZone Director
(E-mail address)

Power Coach
Job Description

Pre-Camp Responsibilities

▼ Develop a rainy day schedule, if your practices are held outdoors. You may consider using instructional or highlight videotapes as an option.

▼ With the help of the PowerZone Director, recruit a coaching staff to work with you. If you recruit help for the week, please be sure to inform the Camp Director.

▼ Contact Camp Director with equipment needs. You will work with the Director in acquiring the needed equipment for your sport.

▼ Contact coaching staff before camp to talk through practice schedule. You may also want to ask for their assistance in locating equipment.

▼ Develop any printed material that you may want to give your coaching staff, including drills and motivational words.

On-Site Responsibilities

▼ Introduce the daily Power Boost. Huddle Leaders will assist campers in completing the devotionals.

▼ Plan and lead two practice sessions each day. Each session lasts about an hour and a half. Remember to plan for as much participation as possible during the practice sessions—skills, drills and competition rather than lecture.

▼ Give directions to Huddle Leaders who serve as your assistants. They will take on an active role in teaching and coaching during your practices. They are there for your help. Use them to help give the campers the one-on-one attention they need.

▼ Have all equipment and facilities ready to go each day to begin practice sessions on time.

▼ We also welcome and encourage you to participate in as much of the PowerZone schedule as possible!

▼ Be sure that all equipment used during your practices is stored properly during the week and that all water coolers are returned to the training room by an adult.

Post-Camp Responsibilities

▼ Be sure that all equipment used during your practices is returned to its rightful owner and that the field area is cleaner than when you arrived.

▼ During Friday's PRO-FILE time be available and ready to present certificates and a challenge to your campers. Certificates are provided by the Camp Director. Be sure to pick them up from the Camp Director.

▼ Complete a Camp Evaluation Form. And attend the Post-Camp debriefing session, which occurs immediately following camper pick-up on the last day of PowerZone.

Recruiting Huddle Leaders

Recruiting Huddle Leaders is an important task. College students and mature, responsible high school juniors and seniors are recommended as great PowerZone recruits. High School sophomores and freshmen may be used as Junior Huddle Leaders to assist Huddle Leaders throughout the week. Remember that each Huddle Leader is responsible for each member of the Huddle for each day of Camp. It is vital that you are confident in your Huddle Leaders' abilities. Remember that you will see the campers' parents each day! Recruit and choose great Huddle Leaders.

On the next page is a sample letter to your Huddle Leaders on PowerZone Letterhead. Be sure that each Huddle Leader has given you a completed Ministry Leader Application (p. 52). Power Huddle Tips (p. 51) will give your Huddle Leaders the keys to leading a successful Huddle. Be sure that your Huddle Leaders attend Huddle Leader Training prior to camp. (Power Leader Training Flyer is on page 56.)

PowerZone 2006 is here! We are excited to announce our PowerZone day camp for 8- to 12-year-old boys and girls surging through this area (dates). I would like to extend to you the exciting opportunity of applying to be a HUDDLE LEADER at PowerZone 2006. Each POWER day will begin at 8:00 AM and will end at 4:30 PM. We already have some of the area's top coaches and athletes scheduled for this week. A surprise athlete will also attend our PRO-FILE time to share about his or her faith each day. Below is the POWER SCHEDULE for each day.

You have been given this invitation because we believe that you could be a vital part of the PowerZone Team in reaching others for Christ. You have been asked to apply for the HUDDLE LEADER position because of your leadership ability and your desire to serve God and reach others.

Please look closely at the enclosed materials and prayerfully determine if this is where God would have you serve. If you discover that this is where God would have you serve, have the two reference letters and application completed and then mail them back to me by (date). If you have any questions, please do not hesitate to contact me. We are looking forward to serving with you at PowerZone 2006!

POWER SCHEDULE	
8:30	Warm-Up
9:00	Power Boost
9:15	Practice
10:45	Huddle
11:30	Lunch
12:00	Recreation
12:45	Huddle
1:15	Practice
2:45	Snack
3:15	Pro-File
4:00	Pick 'em Up

Your Name
PowerZone Director
(E-mail address)

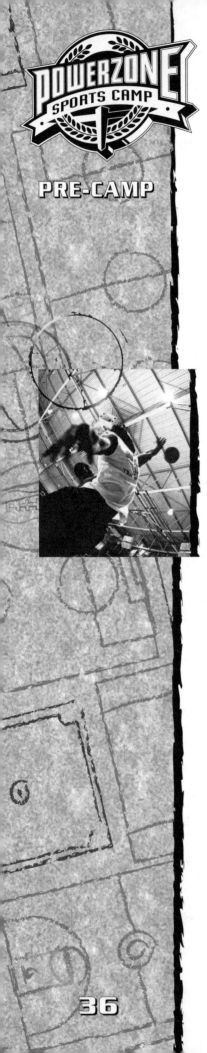

Information for the Huddle Leader Coordinator

▼ Huddle Leaders must be at least 16 years old. Preferably, they are local students who are athletes and want to serve at camp.

▼ Leaders 13 to 15 years old may be Junior Huddle Leaders if they have great references of being mature for their age, responsible, and wanting to serve at camp. A good rule of thumb is that they should be at least four years older than the campers they are supervising. Camp Directors still need to ensure there is the appropriate adult (those over 18 years of age) to camper ratio. The ratio should never get any higher than 1:15.

▼ All Huddle Leaders (Core Staff, Volunteers and Coaches too) must complete and turn in a Ministry Leader Application Form (MLA) to the Huddle Leader Coordinator or Camp Director.

▼ Hold at least two to three Training opportunities for all Huddle Leaders, Junior Huddle Leaders and possibly Coaches. To serve at PowerZone all Leaders must attend one Training session.

At Training:

▼ Try to provide some snacks, drinks and fellowship to begin to mold the group together. Also, begin with some games/ice breakers to help everyone get to know each other.

▼ Have everyone sign in, so you know who was in attendance and who has completed the training.

▼ Go over the Camp Schedule and then go over it again! As you describe the schedule, give the following tips to Huddle Leaders and answer any questions they may have.

　▼ **Warm-up:** Before camp, gather your Huddle by holding up a poster with your Huddle number on it. (Note: Teach Huddle Leaders some games to play with their Huddle as they are waiting for everyone to get there in the morning.) It is important for you to welcome the campers, to make a good impression with your campers' parents, and to be organized.

　▼ **Power Boost:** Set the example and do a quiet time along with your Huddle. Explain in your own words what a quiet time is and what it means to you. Help your campers complete the devotional, find Bible references, etc.

　▼ **Practice:** You are an Assistant Coach to the Head Coach—help them and be involved. Participate in all the drills and help in any way possible. You may need to get more water, take a camper to the bathroom, help clean up the field after practice, etc. Be an assistant with a smile! Also make sure your campers are getting enough water! (Note: Try to take bathroom breaks as a Huddle in between events to cut down on campers missing major parts of the programs.)

▼ **Huddle:** This is the time you need to prepare for—go over the resources we are going to give you and facilitate a biblical discussion with your Huddle. (See Huddle Leader tips—review these tips with them.) Make sure you have played a name game to know everybody else's name—this is very important! Each Huddle should have a designated space where they always have Huddle time—this way the Camp Director knows where everybody is and so do Huddle members in case they get lost. In hot weather, try to provide an air-conditioned classroom if possible.

▼ **Lunch:** Bring your lunch and eat it with your Huddle. Keep the group together. We will provide everyone with a drink—go get those for your Huddle and hand out. Make sure your area gets thoroughly cleaned up by the end of lunch. Make sure trash is thrown away, that everyone had a lunch to eat and that everyone ate something healthy!

▼ **Recreation:** Again, be helpful and be a servant. The Recreation Director should go over the Recreation schedule the morning of or the day before to clue you into what he/she will be trying to accomplish. Find out what you all will be playing and the rules and organize your Huddle. Whatever game it is, have fun with it and be positive. If you think the game stinks—so will your Huddle. Make sure everyone is having a fun time, encourage them to do well and try to keep everyone safe.

▼ **Huddle #2:** Follow up on what you went over this morning, what the Chaplain said, and what the speaker said yesterday. Get your kids talking about the theme of the day and the week. Maybe have your Huddle work on memorizing the camp theme verse, write a rap or a song about the week's theme. Draw them together and create pride within your Huddle. Follow the Bible studies given and you should have no problems.

▼ **Practice #2:** Again, make sure campers are staying hydrated and involved. Report any problems to the Camp Director and/or the Huddle Leader Coordinator. This schedule is not optional, so positively encourage your campers to stay fired up!

▼ **Snack:** Again, go and get snacks and drinks for your Huddle and then hand them out. Make sure your area is nice and clean and get them excited about the guest speaker for the day.

▼ **Pro-File:** You are the role model. If you are enjoying the program, your campers will too. Pay attention, be involved and encourage your campers to listen. Participate in any singing and hang in there—you are almost done for the day!

▼ **Pick-Up:** This can be very chaotic. Try to keep your Huddle under control. Wait for their parents to come and get them from where your Huddle will be seated. Keep them seated and patient. Try to recognize the parents to help them find their campers. Parents have to sign their kids out. Remind parents to do that and show them where to go.

▼ Go over their Huddle Leader Notebook. (Contents listed on the next page.)

▼ Go over Camp Rules (listed in Camp Program).

▼ Go over the Bible passage that will be used for camp. Allow them to get familiar with it and encourage them to use it for their preparation of the Huddle times.

▼ Go over camp theme, daily themes and the Bible studies provided. Remind them that they are responsible for preparing for Huddle time with their campers.

▼ Let them know that they are responsible to keep everyone's name tag, Bibles and water bottles organized each day. Campers will be allowed to take items home after the last session of camp.

▼ If camp starts at 8:30 a.m., Huddle Leaders need to be there no later than 8 a.m. for a morning devotional and meeting, lead by you, the Huddle Leader Coordinator. On the first day of camp, Huddle Leaders need to be there at 7 a.m. to help set up Registration, hang up banners, etc. If pick up is at 4 p.m., the Huddle Leaders can probably go home by 5 p.m. They need to help get their kids picked up, clean up the school or church, and have a Huddle Leader Meeting with the HLC. At this meeting, go over funny quotes and stories of the day, prayer requests, Recreation games for tomorrow and take care of any troubles that may be brewing. Close in prayer and send them home to rest.

▼ If possible, plan a Huddle Leader Party on the last or next to last day of camp. See if you can get some food donated or buy them pizzas. Have it where you are having camp or at a nearby home. (Perhaps a member of your church has a home with a ping pong table, pool table, pool, etc.) Celebrate what God is doing at camp, honor them and thank them for serving.

▼ Confirm that everybody has transportation to and from camp. Make notes of any doctors appointments or issues/conflict Huddle Leaders may have during camp.

Huddle Leader Notebook Contents:

In addition to assembling a notebook with the items listed below, make extra copies of the Daily Themes, Power Boosts and Bible Studies to be taken home in a folder or notebook and studied. Don't let them take the complete Huddle Leader Notebook home for fear of losing it and/or forgetting to bring it back. (Notebooks can also be made for Junior Huddle Leaders if desired.)

▼ Camp Schedule

▼ Camp Rules

▼ Daily Themes, Power Boosts, Bible Studies

▼ Huddle Roster (to be updated each day)

▼ Huddle Leader Tips

▼ Game ideas to play with Huddle

▼ Contact information and cell phone numbers of all Core Staff and Medical Staff

Huddle Leader Needs Checklist:

▼ Huddle Leader Notebook (not to be taken home)

▼ Huddle number poster board sign

▼ Backpack/pillow case to carry Bibles for Huddle time

▼ Black permanent marker to make sure names are written on Bibles, clothes, shin guards, etc. Label everything possible for your campers. (Remind them to take their own stuff home each night!)

▼ Bibles for each camper

▼ Wristwatch

▼ Daily Lunch

▼ Game Ideas: Teach and play with them to allow them to feel comfortable participating

▼ Pens or pencils for Huddle members

▼ Water bottle for each Huddle member with names written in permanent marker

▼ Name tag for each Huddle member

Ideas for Pre-Camp Training:

▼ The day before camp starts, have all staff involved (Huddle Leaders, Junior Huddle Leaders, Coaches, Volunteers, etc.) meet at the place you are holding camp and pray. Pray as a large group and then break everybody up to pray over the school, church, fields, etc. This is also a good time to answer any last questions and to get your team fired up for a GREAT week of camp!

▼ Regularly e-mail or somehow contact your Huddle Leaders to encourage them to pray for camp. Be available for questions and make sure everybody has transportation to and from camp.

Benefits of Being a PowerZone Huddle Leader:

▼ Become a positive role model in your community and kids will love you!

▼ Know that you have made a positive impact in the Kingdom of Christ!

Enrollment Confirmation Form

Campers and their parents will want confirmation of their enrollment in your camp as soon as possible. Be sure to confirm their enrollment soon after your office receives their Registration Form and deposit for PowerZone. When developing your Enrollment Confirmation Form, the following information is important:

▼ Time Registration begins the first day of camp

▼ Place where they are to begin and end their camp experience each day

▼ Necessary items to bring and not to bring

▼ Importance of completing payment before camp begins

▼ Importance of completing their Medical Release Form before camp begins

▼ Importance of completing a Pick-Up Form for the week (This is a Form that gives the name and phone number of the person who has permission to take their child from camp at the end of each day.)

It is important to note that you should not let a camper begin camp without the completion of payment, Medical Release Form and Pick-Up Form.

Idea:

Include a note for parents to place in an easily accessible location (like the refrigerator) with the Daily Schedule, contact numbers and other important information.

The following Enrollment Confirmation Form is a sample of the form you can create. Be sure to note all of the important information on the sample Enrollment Confirmation Form. The Enrollment Confirmation Form is a tri-fold design for printing on 8½" x 11" paper. On the CD-ROM included in this manual, you will find Enrollment Confirmation Forms (both color and black and white) in the following formats:

TIFF — This format is great for your in-office printing and design.

JPEG — This format is great for use on your website.

EPS — This format is used by professional printers.

Enrollment Confirmation

Thomas Jefferson High School

1234 North Street, Anytown, USA

June 20–June 24

church address

ATTENTION

POWER CAMPER AND POWER PARENT

We are excited to have you "plugged in" for PowerZone 2006! This will be an electrifying week of fantastic sports, new friends, faith, fun and foundational training from coaches and athletes. It will be an incredible week that will give you a "jolt" that you will never forget! This brochure is very, very important! Please take the time to read it thoroughly. We do not want you to be disconnected at any time during this powerful week.

POWER FORMS

Located on the other side of this brochure is the Pick-up Form. We will keep a list of who is allowed to pick up your child. If a name is not on this list, we will not release your child to that person unless otherwise given written permission by you, the Power Parent. Please complete the Power Pick-up Form (so that we may return your child to you each day) and the Medical Release Form that is enclosed. You must have the forms completed and turned in before your camper enters PowerZone 2006!

PICK-UP Form *

POWER CAMPER

MONDAY

church _____

sport _____

phone _____

phone _____

name _____

TUESDAY

phone _____

name _____

WEDNESDAY

phone _____

name _____

THURSDAY

phone _____

name _____

FRIDAY

phone _____

name _____

SIGNATURE _____

The above have my permission to pick up my child from PowerZone the week of (dates). _____

*Please be sure to turn in this form at registration.

PowerZone ARRIVAL

Power Registration begins on (date and time). Tuesday through Friday you may drop off your Power Camper at 8:00 a.m. at (location). At the beginning of each Power Day, you will drop off your camper (in the front of the school). Pick-up will also be at the same Power Station at 4:00 p.m. each day. Please be at the Power Station on time!

PowerZone DIRECTIONS

(directions or map to location)

Power Day—Power Parents Invited!

On Friday afternoon, (date), we would like to invite all Power Parents to be Power Campers. Come during lunch at 11:30 a.m. (don't forget to bring your lunch!), and stay until the Pro-File. Be ready for an electrifying day of PowerZone!

POWER ITEMS— DON'T FORGET!

Sunblock, Water Bottle, Permission Form, Power Fees, Pick-up Form

---

POWER NOTICE!

POWER BILL

Your Power Bill comes to a total of (amount). The unpaid amount is due on the first day of PowerZone at registration. Cancellations can be made before (date). All fees, except a $25 service fee, will be refunded in August.

POWER CLOTHING AND EQUIPMENT

Come dressed in sports attire and ready for a Power Workout. Game equipment such as balls will be provided. Bring personal gear such as specific shoes, cleats, sticks, rackets, etc. If you bring cleats, then bring another pair of tennis shoes for after workouts. You will want to bring your own water bottle and sunblock. Do not bring jewelry, radios, CD players or other expensive items.

POWER LUNCH AND SNACK

Each Power Camper is responsible for his/her own lunch. Campers will need to bring a sack lunch, but drinks will be provided. All of the campers will meet in the same room for lunch and snack. Each practice field will have a cooler of water available to campers.

© 2006 Gospel Light. Permission to photocopy granted. *PowerZone Coach's Manual*

Enrollment Confirmation

church address

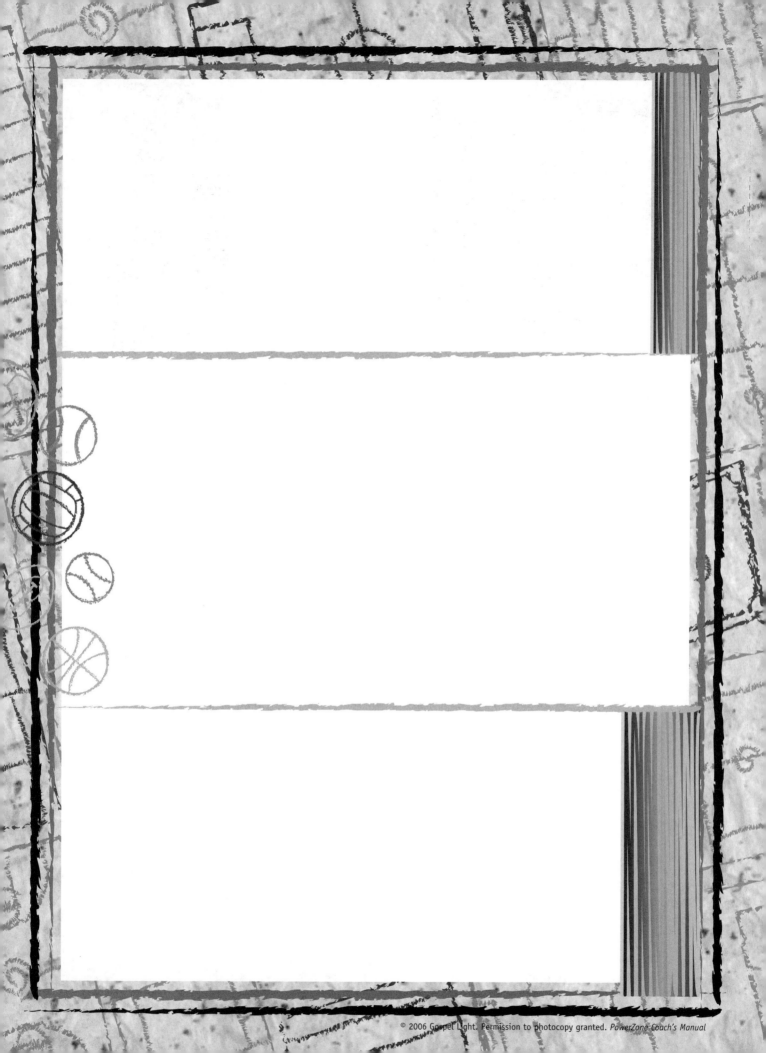

Parent Letter

Parents of campers will want to be included in the PowerZone experience. A letter with several Registration Forms is key in publicizing your camp. Ask parents to pass out the Registration Forms to their student's sports team, their neighbors, their friends. Parents of campers are a great resource for spreading the great news of your PowerZone.

The following page is a sample letter to your camper's parents or guardian on PowerZone Letterhead. On the CD-ROM included in this manual, you will also find a sample letter to your parents on PowerZone Letterhead.

Dear POWER PARENT,

PowerZone is here! We are excited to announce a day camp packed full of friends, foundations in your sport and faith, and fun, fun, fun for everyone! PowerZone 2006 will surge through this area (dates) at (location).

Each POWER day will begin at 8:30 AM and will end at 4:00 PM. We already have some of the area's top athletes and coaches scheduled for this week. A surprise athlete will also attend our PRO-FILE time to share about his or her sport and faith each day. Your 8 to 12 year old will not want to miss one incredible day of PowerZone!

Below you will find the POWER SCHEDULE for the week. If you have any questions, please do not hesitate to contact me. Enclosed are three registration forms. Please feel free to copy these forms to give to friends. Send your camper's Registration Form in as soon as possible along with his or her choice of sport. Spaces are limited! We are looking forward to seeing you and your camper at PowerZone 2006!

Your Name
PowerZone Director
(E-mail address)

POWER SCHEDULE	
8:30	Warm-Up
9:00	Power Boost
9:15	Practice
10:45	Huddle
11:30	Lunch
12:00	Recreation
12:45	Huddle
1:15	Practice
2:45	Snack
3:15	Pro-File
4:00	Pick 'em Up

Name Tags

Name Tags are a lifesaver. These Name Tags are created so that they are easily attached to lanyards—like a concert back-stage pass. The Name Tags have been renamed as the On-Field Pass".

Name Tag Tips:

1. Name Tags should have rounded corners so that campers do not use them as weapons.

2. Print Schedule on the back of the Name Tag. This will help with the question "What's next?"

3. Get the Name Tags laminated. Use a thick laminate so that the Name Tags are not easily destroyed.

4. Since Name Tags are laminated, your Registrar may write camper names and Huddle numbers directly on the Name Tags with a marker.

5. Instruct Huddle Leaders to gather Name Tags at Practice and at the end of each day.

6. Let campers take their Name Tags home at the end of camp.

7. Actual Name Tag size is about 3.5" x 2.5".

The following On-Field Passes are a sample of the Name Tags that you can create. These Name Tags can be printed directly from your computer. A back with sample schedule is included. Use the back of the blank Name Tags to create a Name Tag with your own camp's Schedule. On the CD-ROM included in this manual, you will find Name Tags in the following formats:

TIFF — This format is great for your in-office printing and design.

JPEG — This format is great for use on your website.

EPS — This format is used by professional printers.

If you only need to print a few of these, place the TIFF image on a new document in Word. Then add your local information and print.

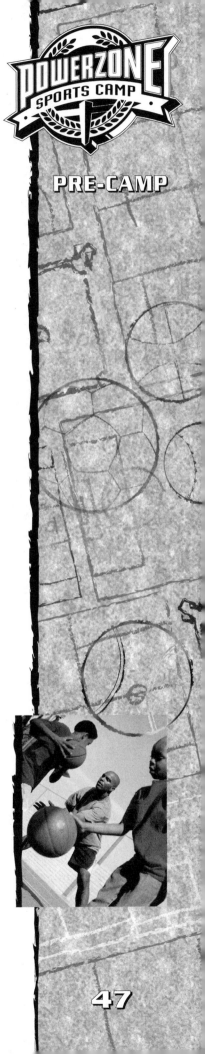

PRE-CAMP

47

ON-FIELD PASS

ON-FIELD PASS

ON-FIELD PASS

ON-FIELD PASS

ON-FIELD PASS

ON-FIELD PASS

ON-FIELD PASS

ON-FIELD PASS

ON-FIELD PASS

TRAINING SCHEDULE

8:30	Warm-Up	12:00	Recreation
9:00	Power Boost	12:45	Huddle
9:15	Practice	1:15	Practice
10:45	Huddle	2:45	Snack
11:30	Lunch	3:15	Pro-File
		4:00	Pick 'em Up

TRAINING SCHEDULE

8:30	Warm-Up	12:00	Recreation
9:00	Power Boost	12:45	Huddle
9:15	Practice	1:15	Practice
10:45	Huddle	2:45	Snack
11:30	Lunch	3:15	Pro-File
		4:00	Pick 'em Up

TRAINING SCHEDULE

8:30	Warm-Up	12:00	Recreation
9:00	Power Boost	12:45	Huddle
9:15	Practice	1:15	Practice
10:45	Huddle	2:45	Snack
11:30	Lunch	3:15	Pro-File
		4:00	Pick 'em Up

TRAINING SCHEDULE

8:30	Warm-Up	12:00	Recreation
9:00	Power Boost	12:45	Huddle
9:15	Practice	1:15	Practice
10:45	Huddle	2:45	Snack
11:30	Lunch	3:15	Pro-File
		4:00	Pick 'em Up

TRAINING SCHEDULE

8:30	Warm-Up	12:00	Recreation
9:00	Power Boost	12:45	Huddle
9:15	Practice	1:15	Practice
10:45	Huddle	2:45	Snack
11:30	Lunch	3:15	Pro-File
		4:00	Pick 'em Up

TRAINING SCHEDULE

8:30	Warm-Up	12:00	Recreation
9:00	Power Boost	12:45	Huddle
9:15	Practice	1:15	Practice
10:45	Huddle	2:45	Snack
11:30	Lunch	3:15	Pro-File
		4:00	Pick 'em Up

TRAINING SCHEDULE

8:30	Warm-Up	12:00	Recreation
9:00	Power Boost	12:45	Huddle
9:15	Practice	1:15	Practice
10:45	Huddle	2:45	Snack
11:30	Lunch	3:15	Pro-File
		4:00	Pick 'em Up

TRAINING SCHEDULE

8:30	Warm-Up	12:00	Recreation
9:00	Power Boost	12:45	Huddle
9:15	Practice	1:15	Practice
10:45	Huddle	2:45	Snack
11:30	Lunch	3:15	Pro-File
		4:00	Pick 'em Up

TRAINING SCHEDULE

8:30	Warm-Up	12:00	Recreation
9:00	Power Boost	12:45	Huddle
9:15	Practice	1:15	Practice
10:45	Huddle	2:45	Snack
11:30	Lunch	3:15	Pro-File
		4:00	Pick 'em Up

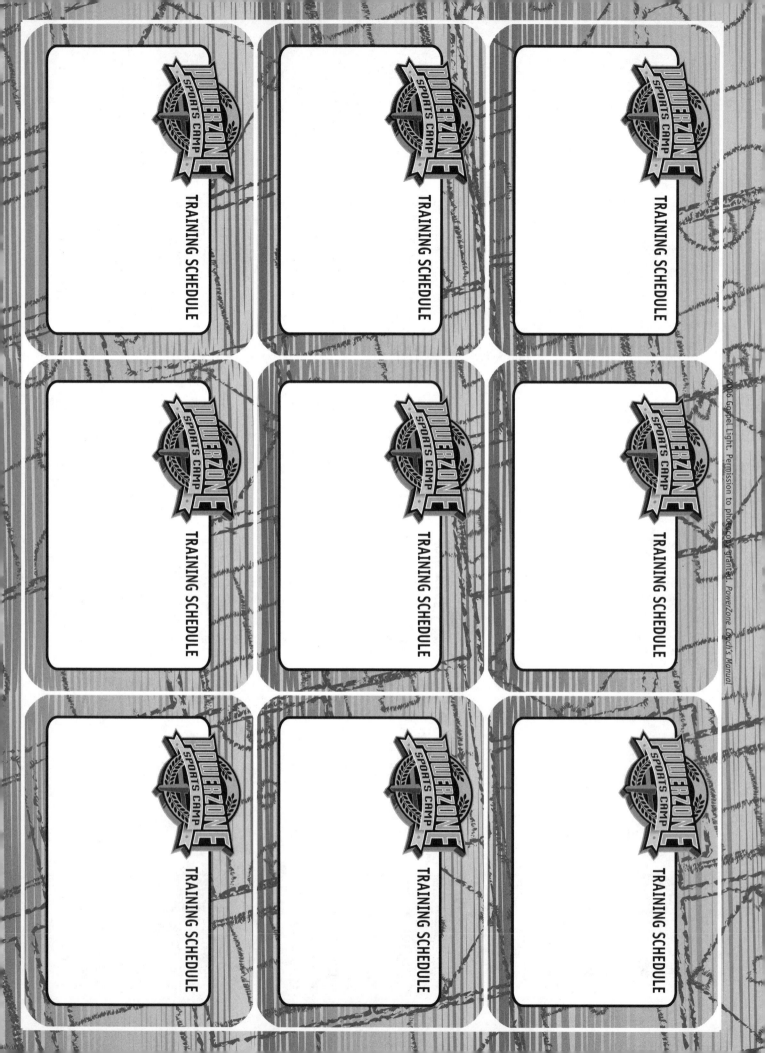

TRAINING SCHEDULE

TRAINING SCHEDULE

TRAINING SCHEDULE

TRAINING SCHEDULE

TRAINING SCHEDULE

TRAINING SCHEDULE

TRAINING SCHEDULE

TRAINING SCHEDULE

TRAINING SCHEDULE

Power Huddle Tips for Leaders

PRE-CAMP

▼ Be on time, set a good example and be a good role model.

▼ Bring your WATCH!

▼ Bring a LUNCH and WATER BOTTLE, too!

▼ Respect your elders and your campers. (Your campers are watching you.)

▼ Ask open-ended questions and don't be afraid of silence. Encourage everyone to participate.

▼ Don't combine two questions in one; make your questions simple.

▼ Facilitate discussion—don't be the center of attention—you're there to help them learn more about Christ.

▼ Don't emphasize your own viewpoint and expect everyone to be impressed by stuff that impresses you. PowerZone is about Jesus, so avoid denominational/theological discussion and point everything back to Christ.

▼ Read/study the material. If you feel comfortable with what you are teaching, your lessons will go smoother.

▼ Summarize main ideas and review and then repeat. Give them life applications and try to meet campers where they are—stretch them all even if you have to use "baby steps" with some.

▼ You're in charge; be clear about what you want them to do and ask them if they understand your directions.

▼ Keep good communication with Staff and your Huddle Leader Coordinator—tell us information even if you don't think we need to know. (Injuries, comments made by campers, etc.)

▼ Use good judgment and common sense. Parents are trusting us with their children.

▼ PRAY, PRAY, PRAY. Pray for patience, God's presence, good weather, protection, for God to use YOU, and for a good time!

▼ God has YOU here in His perfect timing. Be teachable and useable. He has GREAT plans for you and your Huddle!!!

Thank you for serving—you are a blessing!

Ministry Leader Application

Qualifications

▼ A personal relationship with Jesus Christ
▼ A growing faith
▼ Actively involved in the church
▼ An athlete
▼ A team player and a servant

Expectations

▼ Attend Pre-Camp Training Session

▼ Assist during Camp Registration

▼ Monitor your Huddle's needs

  ▼ Be responsible for Huddle members at all times

  ▼ Keep Huddle on schedule

  ▼ Maintain group and individual discipline

  ▼ Eat meals with your Huddle

  ▼ Enforce PowerZone rules

  ▼ Be available to counsel Huddle members if necessary and refer individuals with counseling needs to the appropriate staff persons

▼ Lead Huddle Times

  ▼ Guide discussions involving all Huddle members using the Bible Study material that is provided

  ▼ Guide the Huddle in prayer

▼ Participate in Practices/Recreation Time

  ▼ Serve as a coach/instructor as directed by the head coach

  ▼ Be a Christlike example during competition

Application Process

Please return the application postmarked no later than (date) to the church office.

Thank you for reading the previous information and for taking the time to complete the following application. Your application and recommendations will be prayerfully read as we consider you for a position on the PowerZone Staff as a Huddle Leader.

Huddle Leader Application

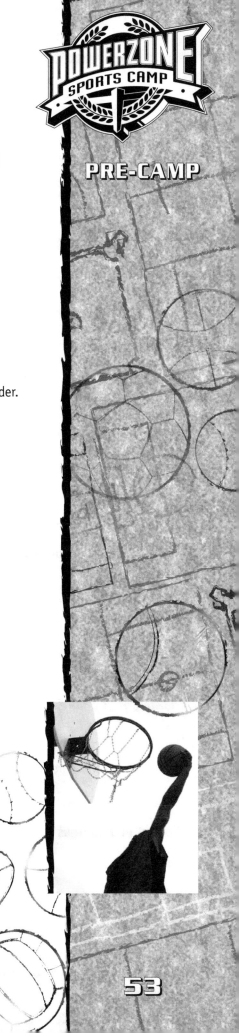

PRE-CAMP

We Are Looking for Volunteers Who...

...are believers in Jesus Christ.

...are seeking an obedient walk with Christ.

...are desiring to serve Christ through their gifts and abilities.

...are active in a local church.

...are wanting to minister to athletes and coaches.

...are athletically focused.

Complete this application if you are interested in being a PowerZone Huddle Leader.

Personal Information

Sex: ❏ M   ❏ F

Name _____
      last   first   middle initial

Home address _____

City _____ State _____ Zip _____

Home phone _____ School/Work phone _____ Cell phone _____

Personal e-mail _____ Secondary e-mail _____

Describe why you are interested in serving at PowerZone

_____

Spouse _____

Children _____

Do you have a current driver's license?   Yes ❏   No ❏ License number _____

1. Are you currently under a charge or have you ever been convicted of any crime?   Yes ❏   No ❏

2. Are you currently under a charge or have you ever been accused or convicted of child abuse or of any crime involving actual or attempted sexual misconduct or sexual molestation of a minor?   Yes ❏   No ❏
If yes, please explain

_____

Are you currently under a charge or have you ever been accused or convicted of possession/sale of controlled substances or of driving under the influence of drugs or alcohol?   Yes ❏   No ❏   If yes, please explain

_____

Is there any other information that we should know?

_____

School or Business Information

School/Business _____

Address _____

City _____ State _____ Zip _____

Athletic Experience

Playing experience (sport, level, years)

_____

_____

Coaching experience (sport, level, years)

_____

_____

Church Experience

1. Please write a brief statement of how you became a Christian.

_____

_____

Are you a member of (name of church)?   No ❏   Yes ❏   For how long? _____

Please list other churches where you have regularly attended over the past five years.

_____

_____

Personal References

Name _____

Address and Phone _____

Name _____

Address and Phone _____

Applicant's Statement

The information contained in this application is true and correct to the best of my knowledge. I authorize any of the above references or churches to give you any information that they may have regarding my character and fitness to work with youth or children.

Signature _____

Date _____

Power Leader Training

YOU MUST ATTEND ONE OF
THE FOLLOWING MEETINGS:

Thursday, June 9, 2006

Monday, June 13, 2006

Thursday, June 16, 2006

From 7-9 PM at the Church Auditorium

Please call or e-mail me to register for the meeting you will be attending.

Power Leader Training

YOU MUST ATTEND ONE OF
THE FOLLOWING MEETINGS:

Thursday, June 9, 2006

Monday, June 13, 2006

Thursday, June 16, 2006

From 7-9 PM at the Church Auditorium

Please call or e-mail me to register for the meeting you will be attending.

Power Leader Training

YOU MUST ATTEND ONE OF
THE FOLLOWING MEETINGS:

(date)

(time)

(location)

(contact)

Power Leader Training

YOU MUST ATTEND ONE OF
THE FOLLOWING MEETINGS:

(date)

(time)

(location)

(contact)

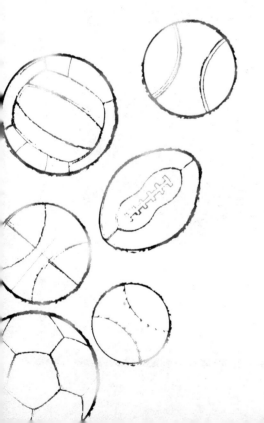

Parents' Day

PowerZone is a great way to involve parents or guardians in the week's excitement. It is also a great way to introduce parents or guardians to the ministry of your church.

Designate one day of PowerZone as Parents' Day. Advertise Parents' Day in the Enrollment Confirmation packet and hand out invitations to campers at Pick-Up a couple of days before Parents' Day. This camp experience for adults works best if the adults are invited for half of the day of camp. For example, adults may arrive to enjoy lunch with their campers and then participate in Recreation, Practice, Snack time and Pro-File time. Be sure to inform your campers' adults to dress appropriately for the day of camp. Also, be sure that your entire Camp Staff knows when and what to expect on Parents' Day.

The following is a sample invitation to campers' parents and guardians for Parents' Day. The invitation is a TIFF image that can be placed in a Word document, and then your local information added. The TIFF is on the CD-ROM included in this manual.

CAMP PROGRAM

Inviting All Parents to Power Day

You're invited to attend PowerZone with your camper on the last day of Camp.

Friday, June 24, 11:30 AM

Bring your own lunch and join us for Lunch, Recreation, Bible Study, Practice, Snack Time and the "Pro-File." (Don't forget your water bottle and sneakers.)

IT WILL BE A POWER-FUL DAY!

Inviting All Parents to Power Day

You're invited to attend PowerZone with your camper on the last day of Camp.

Friday, June 24, 11:30 AM

Bring your own lunch and join us for Lunch, Recreation, Bible Study, Practice, Snack Time and the iPro-File." (Don't forget your water bottle and sneakers.)

IT WILL BE A POWER-FUL DAY!

Inviting All Parents to Power Day

*IT WILL BE A **POWER-FUL DAY!***

Inviting All Parents to Power Day

*IT WILL BE A **POWER-FUL DAY!***

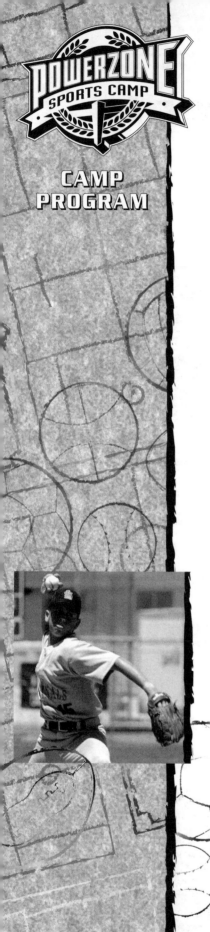

Camper Gifts

Both campers and parents enjoy seeing and remembering their PowerZone experience. A great way to help campers remember their experience and share what they have learned with the adults in their lives is to give the campers something tangible. Camper gifts are a great way to take the PowerZone impact home, and camper gifts can be given to campers each day at minimal cost.

Camper Gift Ideas

▼ New Testament

▼ Stickers

▼ "Christian Youth" magazine

▼ A trading card of a Pro-File Speaker

▼ Christian wristbands (WWJD, etc.)

▼ Devotional Books

Sample Daily Schedule

The following is an example of a PowerZone Schedule. Modify this schedule to fit the program you will provide.

The POWER Schedule*

8:30	Warm-Up (large group assembly)
9:00	Power Boost (devotional time)
9:15	Practice (athletic instruction)
10:45	Huddle (Bible study)
11:30	Lunch
12:00	Recreation (fun games)
12:45	Huddle (Bible study)
1:15	Practice (athletic instruction)
2:45	Snack
3:15	Pro-File (large group assembly)
4:00	Pick-Up

*Parents will begin dropping off their campers early. Because you will need time to prepare and meet with your Staff before camp begins, be sure to inform parents or guardians that your PowerZone Staff will not be available or responsible for their students until 30 minutes prior to the beginning of camp.

Huddle Leader Meeting

Have Huddle Leaders meet one hour prior to the beginning of camp for a devotional, to pray and to talk about the day's events. This will allow the Staff time to be prepared when their campers arrive. Be sure that your campers are in a safe place prior to the beginning of the camp program and that the Huddle Leaders are keeping a close watch on their campers. Encourage Huddle Leaders to be in the same location each day so that their campers can easily locate them. Big signs with each Huddle's number are a big help for campers trying to locate their Huddle.

Warm-Up

Huddles gather in one area to get instructions for the day. Once everyone gathers, this is a good time to go over your Check-In List to make sure that every camper is accounted for. Power Boy and/or Power Girl arrive and do some fun exercises with the entire group. The Team Chaplain (a local youth pastor or children's minister) encourages the group and introduces the day's Theme (See Daily Themes). Encourage the Team Chaplain to use visual aids, especially if you are working with younger campers. End this time by sending campers out to their Practice area for their Power Boost—Devotional. It is suggested that one sport at a time be dismissed—most spirited or quietest sport is allowed to leave first.

*Be sure to go over camp rules on the first day of camp and repeat them as many times as necessary! (See page 68 for suggested Camp Rules).

Power Boost

This is otherwise known as a "Quiet Time" or "Devotional Time." Campers are sent to their Practice location. The Head Coach should be waiting at the Practice loca-

tion with the Power Boost devotionals in-hand. The campers complete the Power Boost on the field or court. This allows the Coach to be involved in their spiritual focus for the day and for the players to relate their faith to the field or court that they will be practicing and competing on. Coaches may want to give their players some time alone to read the devotional, and then call the group together to discuss the Power Boost. (See Power Boost section for daily devotionals.)

Practice

Practice is to be run and organized by the Head Coach and the coaching staff. Be sure to discuss with the Head Coach the equipment and area of space that will be needed for Practice. Check with your Coaches often to see if they are in need of anything. Huddle Leaders are available to assist the Coaches and make sure that their campers understand the instructions being given. Make sure that there is an ample amount of water available for each field and court. Water should be checked before each Practice.

Huddle

A recommended ratio of Huddle Leader to camper is 1:7, especially if working with younger campers. From the moment that the parents check in their campers to the moment that they pick up their camper, the camper is the Huddle Leader's responsibility. After making sure that their Huddle has participated in the morning Warm-Up, completed their Power Boost, and learned in Practice, the Huddle Leader now spends some time in a Huddle. This Huddle time should focus once again on the day's Theme and complete the first half of the day's Bible Study.

Lunch

If you are working with younger campers, it is very important that they eat. Campers are asked to bring their own lunches, while the camp provides the drinks at lunch and at snack. Be sure to ice the drinks at the beginning of each day in a cool area. One idea is to have your campers group their lunches in a designated area during the morning Warm-Up. Remind Huddle Leaders, Coaches and Staff to also bring their lunches. Having campers bring their own lunches ensures that they will have familiar food to eat and is also cost effective for your camp.

Recreation

The entire camp is under the direction of the Recreation Director at this time (a local PE teacher or youth minister is great for this position). This is a good time for relay races, tag games, etc. It can be used as a time of organized recess. Have any extra Camp Staff available to assist the Recreation Director. Huddle Leaders should stay with their Huddles.

Huddle

Huddle Leaders should do the second half of the Bible Study at this time. Use this time to focus again on the day's Theme and to relate this Theme to what has happened throughout the day.

Practice

Again, Practice is to be run and organized by the Head Coach and the coaching staff. Be sure that Huddle Leaders are assisting the Coaches and that there is an ample amount of water for the campers and Coaches.

Snack

It is recommended that the snack and drink are provided for each camper. Gather your campers in the same area for snack time as for your Pro-File time. This will allow your campers to finish their snack while the Pro-File part of your program begins. Try to find a snack that is nutritious as well as good—cheese and crackers, granola bars, etc.—and provide water or sports beverages.

Pro-File

Your campers should look forward to this time every day of camp. Start with any announcements—anything that everyone will need to know for the next day. Have a time of singing (a youth or children's minister who relates well to younger students leads songs). Then have a professional or college athlete share about his or her faith and sport. When scheduling a college or professional athlete, realize that the athlete can travel a short distance to serve others for a short amount of time. Professional or college athletes will often feel like this is a good use of their time to give back to the community that supports them. Don't be afraid to ask for their time. It may be the opportunity that they have been looking for to serve. Also, when scheduling your Pro-File speakers try to feature speakers from each sport represented at your camp and have a balance of male and female speakers. After your professional or college athlete shares, allow for a question and answer time with your campers. Before the Pro-File time begins, set out chairs in the back of the room. Many parents or guardians will stop by early to hear from the athletes—this is great relationship-building time. Close with announcements so that any parents in the room may hear and remind their campers. End each Pro-File time with prayer.

Pick-Up

This time should be as organized as possible. For instance, direct all those picking up campers through one door. They will then pick up their campers and sign them out at another door. Use the Pick-Up Form from the Enrollment Confirmation Form to confirm who is picking up each camper.

Important:

If the name of the person picking up the camper is not on the camper's Pick-Up Form for that day's Pick-Up, DO NOT allow the camper to leave with the person. This must be followed and if not followed will place your camp in legal jeopardy. Take this very seriously. An easy and efficient way to facilitate checking-out campers is by creating a spreadsheet for each day's Pick-Up. Have the person picking up the camper sign by his or her name and write phone number by the signature. Do not let Huddle Leaders leave their Huddle until all campers have been properly checked out. Station Staff without a Huddle around doors so that no campers are lost during this time.

Idea:

Each day have a special camper gift outside of the Pick-Up door for campers—stickers, trading cards, wristbands, magazines, etc.

Idea:

Ask the Pro-File speaker to stay after and sign autographs for the campers. Place the speaker outside or away from the Pick-Up area so as not to interfere with Pick-Up procedures and waiting parents or guardians. Let getting autographs be the responsibility and choice of the Parents and Guardians.

Huddle Leader Meeting

Use this time to go over the day's events. Ask if there are any issues that need to be addressed. Brief Huddle Leaders on the next day's activities. Open and close with prayer.

CAMP PROGRAM

PowerZone Rules for Campers

1. Be an encourager. "Do not let any unwholesome talk come out of your mouths, but only what is helpful for building others up according to their needs, that it may benefit those who listen." Ephesians 4:29

2. Leave this place better than you found it. Be responsible and respectful. No cleats inside the building, wipe your feet, throw away all trash. No marking soles, no food/drink in gym, no street shoes in gym, etc.

3. Huddle Leaders know all, so if you don't know something, ask! If you are ever out of their sight, they need to know why. Your Huddle is your family; stay with them. (Take bathroom breaks as a Huddle.)

4. Do not leave campus for any reason.

5. Equipment will be orderly, placed off to the side (in Huddles). No playing with balls in the halls. Save it for the field or court. Respect others in the school. Quiet in the halls.

6. We are here to love you and teach you. For that, you will get 3 chances. The 1st time you break a rule, you will be corrected by your Huddle Leader or Coach. The 2nd time you mess up, you will sit down and have to miss out on what your Huddle is doing. The 3rd time a rule is broken, you will have to answer to the Camp Director who will call your parents.

7. Put all your belongings in a pile with your Huddle. Lunches and bags should all be together and left in the cafeteria.

8. Drink WATER, Drink WATER, and then DRINK some more. BRING A WATER BOTTLE AND FILL IT! We want you to have a healthy and fun week. Help us help you by staying healthy and by staying positive with a smile on your face and on your heart!

9. Name Tags, lanyards, etc. will be taken home after the last session of camp. Huddle Leaders will keep these items for you during camp. Try not to lose your things!

Daily Themes

Having a Theme for each day of camp gives your camp direction. Letting all Camp Staff, Speakers, Coaches and campers know the Theme of the day enables everyone to emphasize the day's Theme throughout daily activities and in their coaching and teaching. The following Daily Themes handout is a great piece to give to all who are involved in your camp. Introduce the Daily Theme in the morning Warm-Up time. A good idea is to have campers and Staff shout the Daily Theme during group times and have the Coaches remind campers of the Daily Theme during practice. Posters with the Daily Themes are also a good way to drive the Daily Themes into campers' memories.

The following page outlines the Daily Themes based on the Camp Theme—Heart of a Winner. The Heart of a Winner Theme is taken from Mark 12:30-31. The Daily Themes may be printed from the CD-ROM included in this manual.

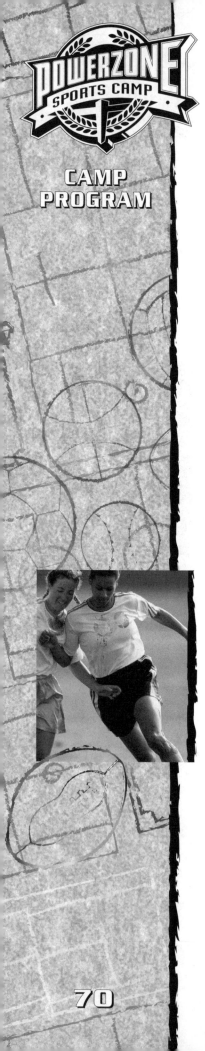

Day 1 Theme

Key Verse: "'Love the Lord your God with all your heart and with all your soul and with all your mind and with all your strength.' The second is this: 'Love your neighbor as yourself.' There is no commandment greater than these." Mark 12:30-31

Objective: Campers will know that it is Jesus who puts hope in our hearts.

Supporting Scripture: Jeremiah 29:11-12; Romans 8:24-25; 1 John 5:12-13

Day 2 Theme

Key Verse: "'Love the Lord your God with all your heart and with all your soul and with all your mind and with all your strength.' The second is this: 'Love your neighbor as yourself.' There is no commandment greater than these." Mark 12:30-31

Objective: Campers will know that it is Jesus who puts endurance in the Heart of a Winner.

Supporting Scripture: Hebrews 12:7; Colossians 1:10-12

Day 3 Theme

Key Verse: "'Love the Lord your God with all your heart and with all your soul and with all your mind and with all your strength.' The second is this: 'Love your neighbor as yourself.' There is no commandment greater than these." Mark 12:30-31

Objective: Campers will know the importance of their actions and that it is Jesus who gives us hearts that do the right things.

Supporting Scripture: James 2:14,17; Luke 6:47-48; 1 John 4:16

Day 4 Theme

Key Verse: "'Love the Lord your God with all your heart and with all your soul and with all your mind and with all your strength.' The second is this: 'Love your neighbor as yourself.' There is no commandment greater than these." Mark 12:30-31

Objective: Campers will know the importance of respect and that it is Jesus who gives our hearts the power to respect others.

Supporting Scripture: Romans 13:6-7; 1 Peter 2:17; Ephesians 4:2

Day 5 Theme

Key Verse: "'Love the Lord your God with all your heart and with all your soul and with all your mind and with all your strength.' The second is this: 'Love your neighbor as yourself.' There is no commandment greater than these." Mark 12:30-31

Objective: Campers will know that Jesus gives our hearts the power to trust during scary times.

Supporting Scripture: Proverbs 3:5-6; John 14:1-3; Psalm 56:3-4

Power Boosts/ Quiet Times

Quiet Times are an essential part of life. Use your Camp Schedule to reinforce the importance of this life skill by designating time in your Daily Schedule for Quiet Times. For campers, however, the thought of being "quiet" is not attractive. Quiet Times have been renamed Power Boosts. There are five Daily Power Boosts. (Note: Each day has a one-word theme—Hope, Endurance, etc. The first letters of these words spell HEART.)

Provide a Bible, a copy of the Power Boost devotional and pen or pencil to each camper every day. While the Head Coach introduces and distributes the Power Boost, Huddle Leaders should be available to guide campers through the devotional as needed.

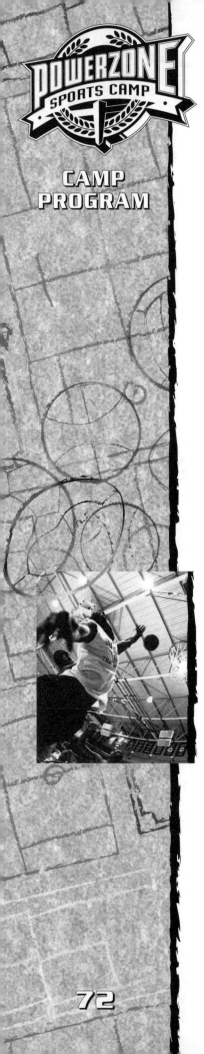

POWERZONE SPORTS CAMP

CAMP PROGRAM

DAY *1* POWER BOOST

H Is for Hope

Introduction

Steve is an excellent football player. He is on the eighth grade team. All he had ever hoped for was for his team to win their league championship. This season, his team was undefeated until the last game, when they met the other undefeated team in the league. Before the game, the team huddled together and said the Lord's Prayer. At the end of the game, Steve's team lost the game.

Did Steve's team lose the game because he did not pray hard enough for the championship? (Campers respond.) God has a plan for you and it is not always what you hope or want to happen.

Pray

Ask God to help you learn and grow through this study. Ask Him to help you have the true Heart of a Winner.

Read Jeremiah 29:11-12

"For I know the plans I have for you," declares the Lord, "plans to prosper you and not to harm you, plans to give you hope and a future. Then you will call upon me and come and pray to me, and I will listen to you."

H Is for Hope

What does it mean to have hope? (Campers respond.)

Hope means believing that something is good. It is to be positive in every situation.

Campers Answer the Following Questions:

1. List something you are hoping for right now. Is there something you hope for in the next 5 to 10 years? (College education, first-place trophy, a car)

2. Does having hope make these wishes come true?

3. What does it mean to have hope in Christ? (Believe that God's plans for you are good, because He loves and cares for you.)

4. What can you do to strengthen your hope in Christ?

Pray

Take time to pray to God and ask Him to help you have a hopeful heart in Christ.

DAY 2 POWER BOOST

E Is for Endurance

Introduction

Sarah is an 8-year-old girl who loves the game of soccer. She had never played the sport, but she loved to watch it on television. For her ninth birthday present, she asked her parents to let her play soccer. Her parents agreed and they signed her up on the local soccer team.

On the first day of practice, Sarah tried really hard to pass the ball and kick it into the goal. She discovered that soccer was a lot harder than it appeared on television. Her body ached from all the running and exercise. Although it was hard, she loved playing soccer. Sarah's parents wondered if Sarah wanted to change her mind about playing soccer. Sarah told them, "I love soccer and it is hard. I know I am not the best player but I want to stick it out. I am not a quitter." Sarah's parents respected her decision.

Pray

Thank God for a new day and ask Him to open your heart and hear what He has for you to discover in this study.

Read Hebrews 12:7

"Endure hardship as discipline; God is treating you as sons."

E Is for Endurance

Endurance means to keep going even when something is hard.

Campers Answer the Following Questions:

1. In a sport, have you ever wanted to quit? Why?

2. Have you ever wanted to quit something but you decided to stay with it? What did you do? How did you feel when it was over?

3. In the verse, what does "endure hardship as discipline" mean to you?

4. Living a life for Christ is not always easy. You have to endure hard times to learn life's lessons. What is your reward for having endurance?

Pray

Thank God for the hard times and ask Him to help you gain the endurance you need to have the Heart of a Winner.

A Is for Actions

Introduction

Have you ever the heard the saying "Actions speak louder than words"? Carmen really wants to be on the volleyball team. That's all she talks about, but she never really practices, plus she eats a lot of junk food. Do you think she will make the team?

People usually remember what people do over what people say. The way you act can please or not please God. God wants us to always act in a way that will glorify Him. Do your actions represent a Christian walk with Christ? It is easier to talk the talk than walk the walk. Actions matter.

Pray

Open in prayer by thanking God for the day. Talk to God about something that is heavy on your heart. He is there for you.

Read James 2:14,17

"What good is it, my brothers, if a man claims to have faith but has no deeds? Faith by itself, if it is not accompanied by action, is dead."

A Is for Actions

Actions mean our behavior—the things we do.

Campers Answer the Following Questions:

1. Have your friends ever asked you to do something that you know you should not do? How did you feel and what was your decision?

2. In the verses, what does it mean when it says "faith without action is dead"?

3. Do you think your actions are pleasing to God? Have you ever acted in a way that was unpleasing to God? How did you feel?

4. What is the most important decision you can make for God today?

Pray

Ask God to help you to always act in a way that will glorify Him. Having the Heart of a Winner in Christ means acting so that others can see Christ through your actions.

POWERZONE
SPORTS CAMP

CAMP PROGRAM

DAY **4** POWER BOOST

R Is for Respect

Introduction

Collin's mom is always telling him to make his bed and clean his room. Collin does not like doing that and he rarely does it. Collin thinks that it is not really important and that his room looks fine the way it is.

His friend Austin comes over to play with Collin's stuff and leaves them on the floor. Collin asks him to help clean up, but Austin does not help. As Collin is asking, he steps on one of his favorite trophies because he didn't see it in all the mess. The trophy breaks.

Pray

Tell God you want to respect others. Tell God you want him to show you how.

Read 1 Peter 2:17

"Show proper respect to everyone: Love the brotherhood of believers, fear God, honor the king."

R Is for Respect

Respect means that you willingly show appreciation for someone. This includes obeying the people God gives to help us (parents, teachers, coaches, etc.).

Campers Answer the Following Questions:

1. Who is showing disrespect in the story about Collin? In what ways are the boys being disrespectful?

2. Why do you think God wants us to show respect to each other?

Pray

Tell God what is keeping you from respecting others. Ask Him to help you put in your heart the things you need to respect others.

DAY 5 POWER BOOST

T Is for Trust

Introduction

JC is walking home from school and a car pulls up alongside him. In the car is a man that JC has never seen. He asks JC to come close to the car because he has some ice cream he wants to give him. What should JC do?

Trust is something gained over time and it means someone will always be there for us. We can trust God because He always loves and cares for us. God is there no matter what happens or what sin we have done. God's love is unconditional, and trusting in Him is a win-win situation. Trust in Him now and forever.

Pray

Thank God for the day and tell Him how much you trust in His Word. Ask Him to open your heart to trust in Christ.

Read Proverbs 3:5-6

"Trust in the Lord with all your heart and lean not on your own understanding; in all your ways acknowledge him, and he will make your paths straight."

T Is for Trust

Trust means to have a firm belief or faith in another.

Campers Answer the Following Questions:

1. Name some people in your life whom you trust.

2. Why do you trust them?

3. What does it mean to trust in the Lord with all your heart?

4. Do you have trust in God? Why?

5. What do you think God is saying to you in these verses?

Pray

Take this time in prayer to share with God anything that is keeping you from trusting in Him.

Bible Studies

The following five Bible Studies are based on the theme Heart of a Winner—Mark 12:30-31. These Bible Studies are to be used for the Huddle time during camp. The Bible Studies are written so that you may use each study for one Huddle time or divide the day's Bible Study to be used for two Huddle times. The Bible Studies may be printed from the CD-ROM included in this manual.

CAMP PROGRAM

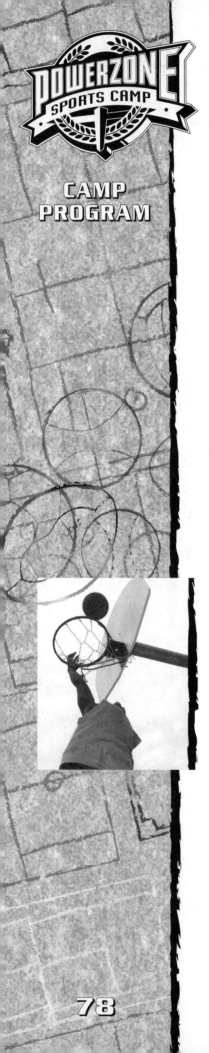

DAY **1** BIBLE STUDY

Key Verse

"'Love the Lord your God with all your heart and with all your soul and with all your mind and with all your strength.' The second is this: 'Love your neighbor as yourself.' There is no commandment greater than these." Mark 12:30-31

Objective

Campers will know that it is Jesus who puts hope in our hearts.

Materials

Bibles, butcher paper, markers and crayons

Warm Up

What Is a Winner?

Have you ever won a race, a game or a tournament? Do you know what it takes to be a winner?

On a sheet of butcher paper, draw an outline of an athlete. Then ask each camper to draw on the outline something that will make that athlete a winner—e.g., fast shoes, big muscles, etc. Option: You could have the campers do this themselves on small sheets of paper.

This week's theme is the Heart of a Winner. We want to discover what is in the Heart of a Winner.

What does your heart have to do with winning?

If we put the best ingredients in our hearts, we will have the best chance to be winners.

Each day, we will be learning something that needs to be in our hearts. We will use the word HEART to help us remember the words.

Today we are going to take the first letter, H. Any ideas about something that starts with H that is in the Heart of a Winner?

Today, H stands for hope. Hope means to believe that something is good. It is having a reason to be positive in every situation.

DAY *1* BIBLE STUDY

Workout

Read Jeremiah 29:11-12

"For I know the plans I have for you," declares the Lord, "plans to prosper you and not to harm you, plans to give you hope and a future. Then you will call upon me and come and pray to me, and I will listen to you."

Everyone find the verses in your Bible. Read them aloud two times.

What does God want to give us? What will He do when we pray to Him?

Read Romans 8:24-25

"For in this hope we were saved. But hope that is seen is no hope at all. Who hopes for what he already has? But if we hope for what we do not yet have, we wait for it patiently."

Everyone find these verses in your Bible and read them two times.

What is the biggest thing you have ever hoped for or wanted? Did it come true? How long did you have to wait?

Group Work

Write Mark 12:30-31 on a sheet of butcher paper and display.

Activity 1

Get in a circle and practice memorizing our key verses, Mark 12:30-31, by going around the circle and having everyone read a word from the verses. Go around the circle until everyone has said each word. Then take the poster down and go around the group and see if anyone can recite the verses.

Activity 2

Get in a circle and take turns acting out the following situations. Have someone act out each situation displaying hope and have another camper act out the same situation without hope.

▼ Playing a game against a tough opponent

▼ Taking a test that is very hard

▼ Trying out for a team that you really want to make

Discuss what it feels like to have hope in those situations and what it feels like to be hopeless.

Warm Down

Read 1 John 5:12-13

"He who has the Son has life; he who does not have the Son of God does not have life. I write these things to you who believe in the name of the Son of God so that you may know that you have eternal life."

Those who have Jesus in their hearts have hope because He loves us and knows what is best for us.

If Jesus is in your heart, you can have hope. Hope is believing in God and knowing He has the ultimate plan for our lives.

Who is the Son of God? (Jesus.)

Having the Heart of a Winner begins with having Jesus in your heart. Jesus gives us hope.

Hope gives us the power to love God with all of our heart, strength and soul.

Have your campers get in a circle. Have the campers talk about what they hope God will do in their lives today, this week and this year. Invite the campers to ask Jesus to be in their hearts and lives if they have never asked him before. Close in prayer.

DAY 2 BIBLE STUDY

Key Verse

"'Love the Lord your God with all your heart and with all your soul and with all your mind and with all your strength.' The second is this: 'Love your neighbor as yourself.' There is no commandment greater than these." Mark 12:30-31

Objective

Campers will know that it is Jesus who puts endurance in the Heart of a Winner.

Materials

Bibles, paper, pencils and deck of playing cards for every two students

Warm Up

Yesterday we talked about a winner. What is a winner? What is in the Heart of a Winner? Why should we have the Heart of a Winner?

Who can tell me our letter and word for yesterday? H for hope. What is hope?

Airplane Flying Contest

Have each camper make a paper airplane and see whose plane can fly the farthest. As the planes are flying through the air, talk about how the planes have endurance to stay in the air.

Endurance Test

Have campers perform different tests of endurance. (Push-ups, sprint in place, stay in a deep knee bend position, etc.) As they are doing these activities, emphasize that endurance is very important to athletes.

Today, our letter is E and it stands for endurance. Does anyone know what it means to endure? It means to continue or keep going even when something is hard. Have you ever gotten tired or had pains from running a lot? What did you do to keep going and endure? To have endurance, you have to train your body to keep going.

DAY *2* BIBLE STUDY

Workout

Read Colossians 1:10-12

"And we pray this in order that you may live a life worthy of the Lord and may please him in every way: . . . being strengthened with all power according to his glorious might so that you may have great endurance and patience, and joyfully giving thanks to the Father."

These verses talk about power and strength, according to His glorious might. Whose glorious might is this verse talking about? What are some examples of Jesus' might? (Creating the universe, healing the sick, rising from the dead.) According to this verse, what does God give us? (Endurance, patience and power.)

Read Hebrews 12:7

"Endure hardship as discipline; God is treating you as sons."

Everyone find these verses in your Bible and read them two times.

In sports, when do you get tired? When you lose, do you ever feel like giving up? Enduring hardship is part of being a disciplined athlete. As Christians, we also will need to endure hardships. When are some times you need endurance?

In sports and in life, God can help us endure. No matter how hard things may get, we must work to live our lives and compete in a way that is pleasing to God. It is Jesus who gives us endurance and we know that He had endurance, because He died on the cross for us.

Group Work

Divide into two groups.

Group 1

You will need pencils and paper. Campers each take a sheet of paper and write memory verses Mark 12:30-31. Right-handed campers must use left hand. Left-handed campers must write with their right hand.

Group 2

Each camper gets a partner. Give each pair a deck of cards. Campers build card pyramids. Take two cards and stand them up leaning against each other. This forms a base. Your pyramid should have four bases on the first level. Then, take one card and lay it across the top of the bases making a floor. The next level will have three bases. Continue this process until there is one base on the top. Hint: If your pyramid falls, start over with a hopeful heart that you can endure and complete the job.

Groups switch activities after several minutes.

Get the Huddle back together and discuss.

What was hard about writing your memory verse with your weak hand? Did you get frustrated? How did you act? Did you want to quit or did you think, "I give up"?

How did you feel when you were building the pyramid? Did you get frustrated? How many times did it fall down?

DAY 2 BIBLE STUDY

Warm Down

These activities show that even when things are bad, we must work through them and endure. It is Jesus who can give us the endurance to make it through the really hard times in life.

To have endurance in our Heart of a Winner, we need to have Jesus in our hearts.

Yesterday, we talked about putting Jesus in our hearts and lives because we need to have Hope to be winners. Today, we want to put Jesus into our hearts so that we can have endurance for everything that comes our way in life.

Do you have Jesus in your heart?

We must not give up when things are hard. We must endure the hard times to be winners. Remember, E is for endurance. Everything happens for a reason. God has good plans for us. Work hard in your sports and in living for Christ. Christ endured the cross for us.

Now grab a pencil and write in your Bible the top three things you want to ask Jesus to give you endurance for. Maybe it is putting up with your brother or sister, maybe endurance to obey your parents, maybe to endure a difficult time like attending a new school.

When you are done, let's get back together and pray for each other.

Close by reciting Mark 12:30-31 and praying together.

DAY 3 BIBLE STUDY

Key Verse

"'Love the Lord your God with all your heart and with all your soul and with all your mind and with all your strength.' The second is this: 'Love your neighbor as yourself.' There is no commandment greater than these." Mark 12:30-31

Objective

Campers will know the importance of their actions and that it is Jesus who gives us hearts to do the right things.

Materials

Bibles, pencils and paper

Warm Up

We have learned the first two letters of HEART. What are they? What do they stand for? (H for Hope, E for Endurance)

Can you guess today's letter? What do you think it stands for? (A for Actions)

What are actions?

Actions mean our behavior—the things we do.

Action Game

We are going to play an action-packed game. We are going to play Red Light, Green Light. (Campers start on a line and teacher yells "Green Light" to let the campers run as fast as they can toward the other side of the room. Teacher yells "Red Light" at various times to have them stop. They get two steps after you yell "Red Light." The first person to get to the other end of the playing area wins.)

DAY **3** BIBLE STUDY

Work Out

Read Luke 6:47-48

"I will show you what he is like who comes to me and hears my words and puts them into practice. He is like a man building a house, who dug down deep and laid the foundation on rock. When a flood came, the torrent struck that house but could not shake it, because it was well built."

Everyone find these verses in your Bible and read them two times.

In the verses, what actions did the man take? His house and foundation were well built because of his actions. God's Word can be the foundation for our lives. God wants our actions to show that He's our strong foundation.

Read James 2:14,17

"What good is it, my brothers, if a man claims to have faith but has no deeds? Faith by itself, if it is not accompanied by action, is dead."

What are some different ways our actions can show our faith in God? What might our brothers and sisters say about our actions? Our moms or dads?

Group Work

Each camper will need to find a quiet place. When they get to their places, they are to do the following:

1. Pray about how they need to change their actions in different parts of their life. Have them write down things they need to stop doing and things they need to start doing.

2. Write down on a sheet of paper how they act around people who don't know Jesus. Write one paragraph about how they should act around these people and how they would share their faith with them.

Give them about 10 minutes and then bring your Huddle back together to share their thoughts about this activity.

Then take a few minutes and talk about some of the actions they have displayed in the last few months that were not pleasing to God. (Examples: gossiping, bad sportsmanship, disrespect, bad attitude.)

Warm Down

Our verse for the week is:

"'Love the Lord your God with all your heart and with all your soul and with all your mind and with all your strength.' The second is this: 'Love your neighbor as yourself.' There is no commandment greater than these." Mark 12:30-31

Having the Heart of a Winner means loving God and showing love to others through our actions.

Read 1 John 4:16

"And so we know and rely on the love God has for us. God is love. Whoever lives in love lives in God, and God in him."

According to the Bible, God is love. If we want to do the right things and act the right way, we need to have love in our hearts. We can do that by having God in our hearts.

The Heart of a Winner is a heart that has God in it. If God is in your heart, you will have the power to love and act the right way.

Referring to the lists the campers wrote earlier, have them pray that God would:

come into their hearts so that they can change their actions

and/or

give them more power to love and do the right thing.

Close by reciting Mark 12:30-31 and by praying together.

DAY 4 BIBLE STUDY

Key Verse

"'Love the Lord your God with all your heart and with all your soul and with all your mind and with all your strength.' The second is this: 'Love your neighbor as yourself.' There is no commandment greater than these." Mark 12:30-31

Objective

Campers will know the importance of respect and that it is Jesus who gives our hearts the power to respect others.

Materials

Bibles, a discarded large ball (soccer ball, basketball, volleyball, football, etc.) for each group of eight campers, pen

Warm Up

H for Hope

E for Endurance

A for Actions

What is the next letter? R for respect.

Respect Role-play

Let's have a little fun. Let's act out different types of respect. Volunteers choose one of the following people to act out.

1. The world's best coach giving the Huddle instructions on a soccer (or basketball, etc.) move

2. The world's strongest police officer pulling over a speeding bus holding the entire Huddle

3. The Army's best hand-to-hand combat trainer teaching the Huddle combat maneuvers

4. A parent teaching a teenager to drive

5. Think of a few of your own.

What does "respect" mean? Why were the authority figures we just acted out worth respecting? Who do you respect?

Work Out

Read Romans 13:6-7

"Authorities are God's servants, who give their full time to governing. Give everyone what you owe him: If you owe taxes, pay taxes; if revenue, then revenue; if respect, then respect; if honor, then honor."

The verses say that authorities are whose servants? Why should we respect them? Who are the authorities in your life? Tell about a time when you respected your parents. Your teacher. Your coach. When is it hard for you to respect someone?

Read 1 Peter 2:17

"Show proper respect to everyone: Love the brotherhood of believers, fear God, honor the king."

Everyone find these verses in your Bible and read them two times.

What does it mean to fear God? (Respect Him, believe in His power.) Having the Heart of a Winner means having respect in your heart for God and for the people in your life.

Group Work

Challenge campers to quickly brainstorm ways to show respect to others (listen while others speak, be patient, pay attention to others' feelings, etc.).

Use a pen to print the campers' answers on a large discarded ball.

Campers stand in a circle and toss ball around the circle.

When you call out "freeze," camper holding ball reads the answer that is closest to his or her left thumb.

Other campers quickly tell a specific time kids their age can show respect to others in that way.

Warm Down

It's easy to show respect to other people when we are getting along and don't have any disagreements. But because we're humans, we sometimes have misunderstandings and disagreements that make it hard to treat others with respect.

Read Ephesians 4:2

"Be completely humble and gentle; be patient, bearing with one another in love."

What attitudes and actions are described in this verse?

What might result from these attitudes and actions?

How might following these verses make a difference in your school? In your neighborhood? In your family? On your sports team?

When we think about God's love for us and for others, it helps us to have Hearts of Winners and remember to show respect to others, even when there are problems.

Ask each camper to think of a problem he or she has had in getting along with another person. Ask the camper to evaluate how well he or she showed respect in the situation.

After several minutes, close in prayer, asking God's help in having the Heart of a Winner and treating others with respect.

Key Verse

"'Love the Lord your God with all your heart and with all your soul and with all your mind and with all your strength.' The second is this: 'Love your neighbor as yourself.' There is no commandment greater than these." Mark 12:30-31

Objective

Campers will know that Jesus gives our hearts the power to trust during scary times.

Materials

Blindfolds—one piece of cloth or bandana for every two campers, large sheet of paper, felt pen, ball, container (box, laundry basket, etc.)

Warm Up

Trust Walk/Mine Field

Every day this week, we have learned a word for each letter of the word HEART. Who can tell me all the letters and words we have learned this week?

H for Hope

E for Endurance

A for Actions

R for Respect

What is today's letter? (T) Can anyone guess today's word?

Today's word is trust. What is trust? Trust means to have a firm belief or faith in another.

What does trust have to do with having the Heart of a Winner?

Each camper gets a partner. One partner will put on a blindfold. The other partner must lead his or her partner around. Campers place the follower's left hand on the leader's right forearm. The leaders tell their partners to turn right or left. Have them walk around for about two minutes. Then, the campers switch places. At the end of this activity, bring your Huddle together.

Optional: Play Mine Field, where one partner guides the blindfolded partner through a mine field (chairs, balls, cones, etc.) to the other side of the room by yelling out instructions. If their partner hits a mine, they blow up and they are done.

DAY **5** BIBLE STUDY

Work Out

Read Psalm 56:3-4

"When I am afraid, I will trust in you. In God, whose word I praise, in God I trust; I will not be afraid."

What is the scariest situation you were ever in? Why were you afraid? How can trusting God help when you're afraid?

Read John 14:1-3

"Do not let your hearts be troubled. Trust in God; trust also in me. In my Father's house are many rooms; if it were not so, I would have told you. I am going there to prepare a place for you. And if I go and prepare a place for you, I will come back and take you to be with me that you may also be where I am."

Do you ever get scared about what will happen when you die? Where did Jesus go after He died and rose again? Why did He go there? What do you think Jesus meant when He said, "Trust in God; trust also in me"? How do you do that?

Group Work

Draw a line down the center of a large sheet of paper. Print "Team 1" on one side and "Team 2" on the other. Divide group into two teams. Teams take turns attempting to toss a ball into a container. Each time the ball lands in the container, team writes a letter of the word "trust" on its side of the paper.

When one team completes the word, the team tells a situation in which a kid might have to show trust in God.

Repeat game as time permits.

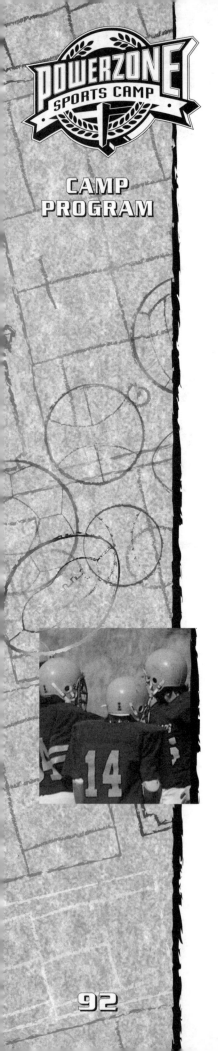

DAY 5 BIBLE STUDY

Warm Down

Read Proverbs 3:5-6

"Trust in the LORD with all your heart and lean not on your own understanding; in all your ways acknowledge him, and he will make your paths straight."

What does it mean to "lean not on your own understanding"?

What does having the Heart of a Winner have to do with this verse?

Describe the actions of someone who is trusting God.

God wants us to trust in Him. When things get hard or tough, talk to God. In the good times, talk to God.

Have campers pray silently to tell God they want to fully trust in Him. Close the prayer time by thanking God for each camper and asking Him to help each one develop the Heart of a Winner.

Camper Certificate

Campers should be recognized for their hard work during camp. Use Camper Certificates to recognize their hard work during camp and to remind them of their camp experience throughout the year. Create the following Camper Certificate on colored (use camp colors) or special paper that will make the Camper Certificate a standout piece. The Camper Certificate can be printed from your computer and is in a WORD document on the CD-ROM included in this manual.

CAMP PROGRAM

This is to certify that

has completed a week of training at

Coach

Coach

Coach

Camp Director

Camper and Staff Evaluation Form

Evaluating your camp will provide an excellent means for improving your camp adventure for your campers and Staff. A thorough review of the camper and Staff Evaluation Forms, plus honest feedback from Staff and Coaches will be immensely beneficial in making your camp the highlight of your community. The Evaluation Form will also provide much needed information for Follow-Up with local churches and sponsoring organizations

The following is a sample Evaluation Form given to campers and Staff. The Evaluation Form can be printed from your computer and is in a WORD document on the CD-ROM included in this manual.

Evaluation

Name _____

Age _____

Sport _____

Church _____

	Excellent	Good	Average	Below Average	Bad
Practice	❏	❏	❏	❏	❏
Huddle Time	❏	❏	❏	❏	❏
Recreation	❏	❏	❏	❏	❏
Speakers	❏	❏	❏	❏	❏
Coaches	❏	❏	❏	❏	❏
Music	❏	❏	❏	❏	❏

If you could add or change one thing at PowerZone, what would it be?

_____

_____

What was your favorite thing about PowerZone this week?

_____

_____

What did you learn this week about God and your sport?

_____

_____

What decision did you make this week?

❏ Became a Christian

❏ Already a Christian, but gave God more control this week.

❏ Other _____

POST-CAMP

Follow-Up

The important task after camp is to keep your campers plugged into the PowerZone experience and to be sure that they are plugged into your church. Follow-Up is essential for your campers' Christian growth. Follow-Up should take place by the church, and the camper's Huddle Leader if applicable.

Ideas

1. Using the information on each PowerZone Evaluation form, determine what follow-up is most appropriate for each camper. Campers who made first-time commitments to Christ or recommitted their lives in some way should be contacted by the children's or youth leaders at your church and invited to participate in regular Bible study, small groups, etc. Suggest that children's or youth leaders, Huddle Leaders and other staff send personal letters to campers after PowerZone concludes. (Note: Letters can be prepared ahead of time and then personalized by leaders.)

2. Create a mailing list of all unchurched families from PowerZone. Give the ministry leaders within your church a copy of the mailing list to send promotions about other church events.

3. Recruit volunteers to call campers and their families in the weeks following PowerZone to tell them of upcoming church events and inquire if they have any questions about the church and its ministry programs.

4. Plan a children's/youth family activity in the month following PowerZone. Distribute a flyer during PowerZone and mail a flyer to each family a week or two prior to the event. Finally, give each family a friendly invitation by phone the week leading up to the event.

5. Suggest that children's and youth leaders from your church (Sunday School teachers, small group leaders, etc.) attend the Parents' Day. Ask Huddle Leaders to introduce leaders to campers and their parents.

6. Take video or digital pictures of campers throughout PowerZone. After camp, have volunteers make and distribute videocassettes or CDs along with a church-ministry brochure.

POST-CAMP

Thank Yous

Thanking those involved with your PowerZone is important. They are a part of the PowerZone family. Be sure to thank all those involved with your PowerZone. Be sure to thank your campers, their parents, your Huddle Leaders, your Staff, your volunteers, the site, and any speakers who gave of their time and talents. The following sample thank-you letter for campers is printed on PowerZone Letterhead. The sample thank-you letter may be printed from the CD-ROM included in this manual.

Hey PowerCamper,

Thank you for being a part of the PowerZone experience. The week was certainly electrifying. We know you will not forget all of the sports, fun, Bible studies and athletes you met. Continue to practice hard, giving it your all every day. Review the different skills that your Coaches taught you.

Keep your Heart of a Winner verses close to you—**Mark 12:30-31**. Say them every day. Remember what the Heart of a Winner is all about:

H – HOPE means believing that Jesus loves you and wants the best for you.

E – ENDURANCE means you need to keep going even when it gets hard.

A – ACTIONS are a sign of what is in our hearts—we must act the way Jesus wants us to act.

R – RESPECT is the willingness to show appreciation to people for how God made them.

T – TRUST means having a firm belief that Jesus can provide the best for you both now and forever.

If you seek Jesus and pour these five themes into your heart regularly, you will have the Heart of a Winner.

Heart of a Winner,

(Your Name)
PowerZone Director

Field Diagrams

On the following pages you will find copies of field diagrams for these sports: baseball, basketball, football, lacrosse, soccer, softball, tennis and volleyball. Field diagrams may be used to show player positions, diagram plays, explain strategy, etc.

Photocopy the diagram(s) for the sport(s) you will provide. Provide copies for coaches and assistant coaches. The diagrams are also provided on the CD-ROM included in this manual.

Baseball

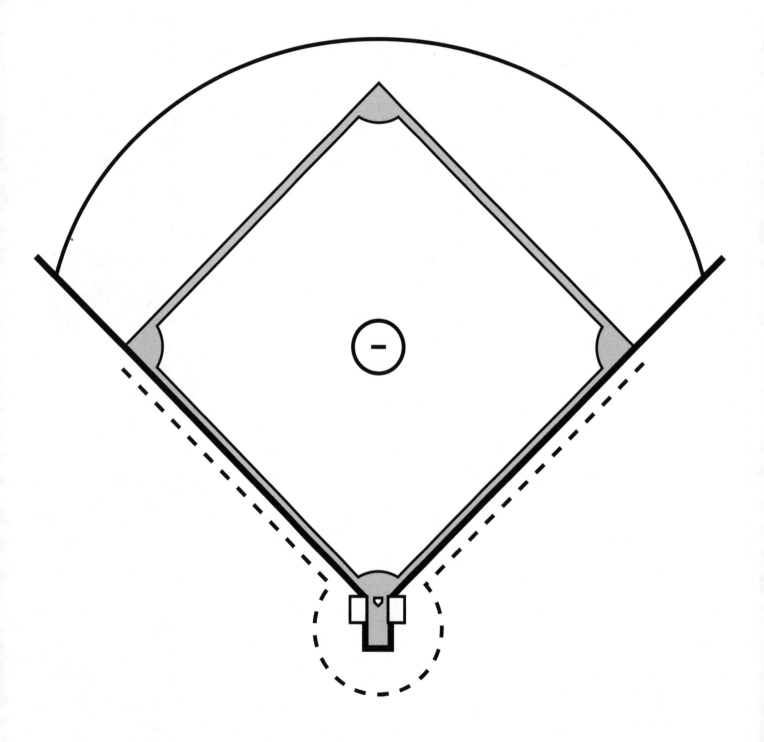

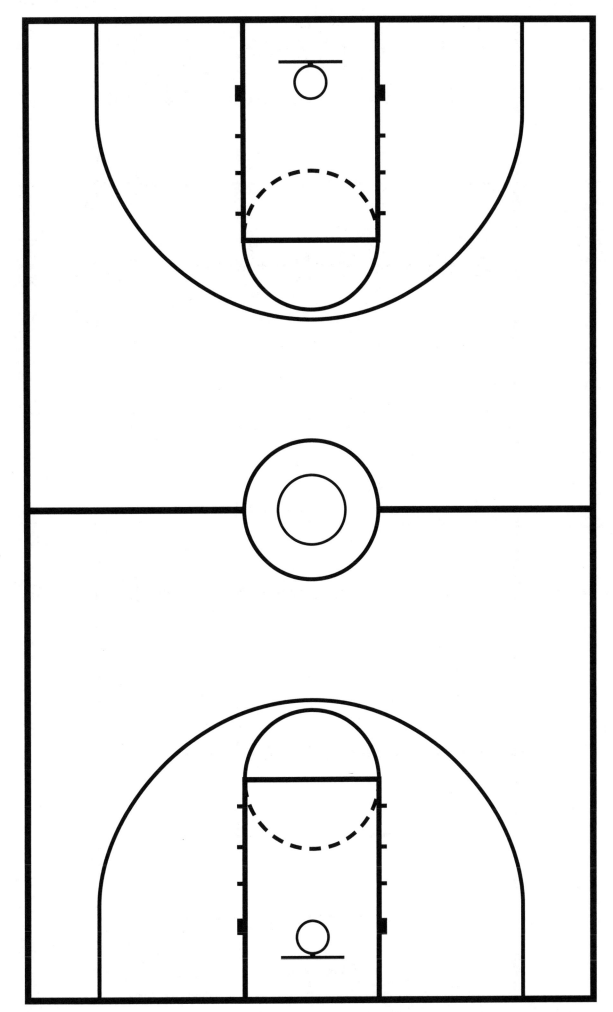

Basketball

Football

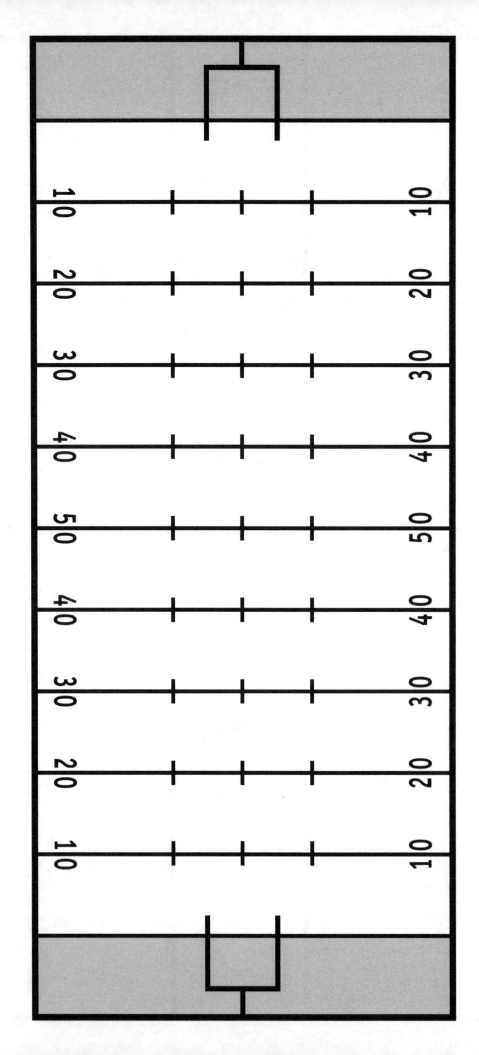

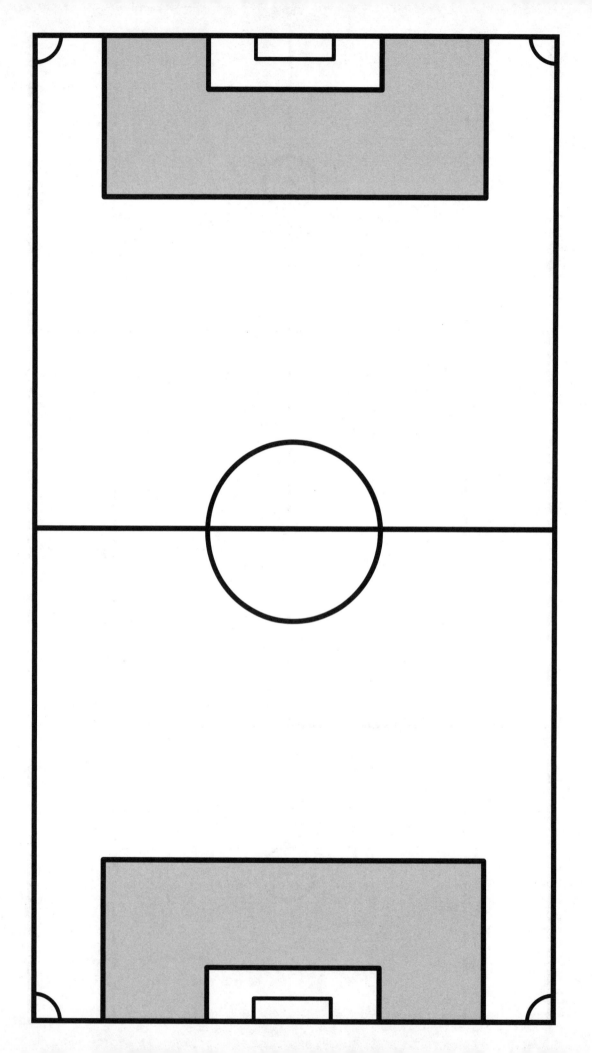

Soccer

Softball

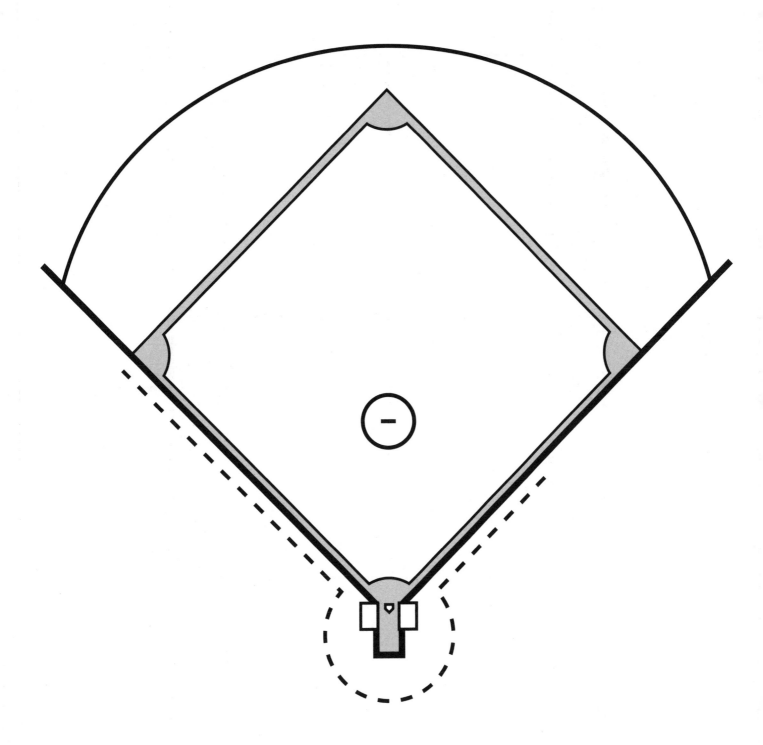

Tennis

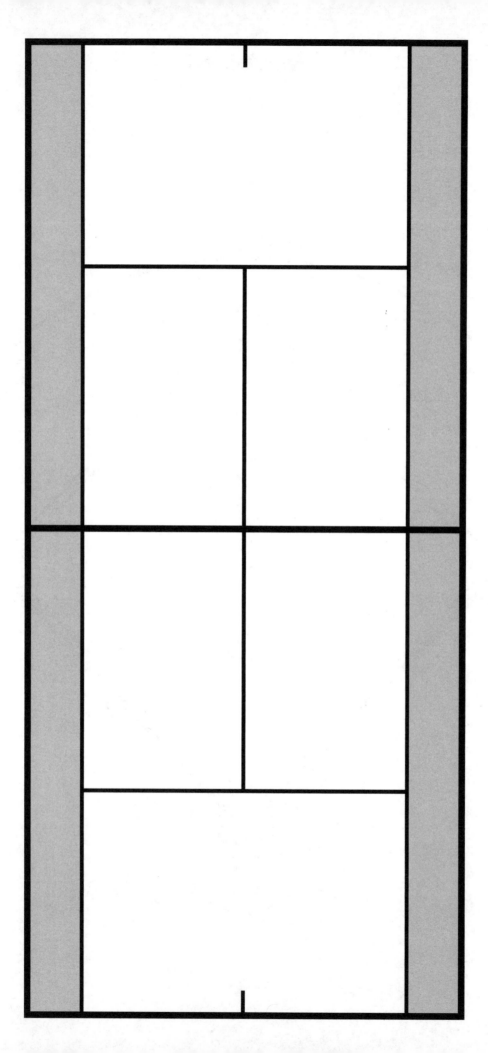

Volleyball

How to Teach Children to Think and Act Like Jesus

"If people do not embrace Jesus Christ as their Savior before they reach their teenage years, the chance of their doing so at all is slim."

George Barna
Transforming Children into Spiritual Champions

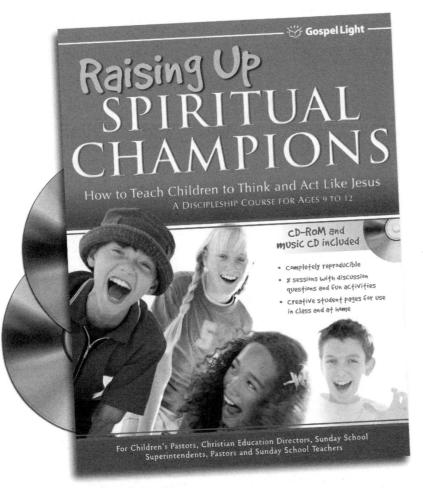

Raising Up Spiritual Champions
How to Teach Children to Think and Act Like Jesus
A Discipleship Course for Ages 9 to 12

Help kids answer the big questions about what it means to think and act like Jesus every day of their lives! This eight-session discipleship program provides the tools teachers need—from meaningful discussion questions to creative activities, from student pages to parent pages—to nurture lifelong spiritual growth in their students. Because most children's spiritual beliefs are in place by age 13, it's crucial that they acquire a biblical foundation for how they view themselves and the world. This program will help leaders teach God's truth during these all-important preteen years!

ISBN 08307.36638
Reproducible Manual
with CD-ROM and Music CD

Raising Up Spiritual Champions Includes

- CD-ROM containing everything in this book, including awards, **Student** and **Parent Pages**, publicity flyers, customizable forms, clip art and more!
- 8 reproducible sessions with discussion questions and fun activities
- Reproducible music CD with 12 praise and session-related songs
- How-tos for setting up the program
- 12 teacher-training articles
- **Student Pages** for use in class and at home to build discipleship habits
- **Parent Pages** that support parents in their role of spiritual teachers
- Teaching resources, including skits, discussion cards, games and more!

Available at your
Gospel Light supplier.

Gospel Light
God's Word for a Kid's World!™

www.gospellight.com

Smart Resources for Your Children's Ministry

Children's Ministry is quickly becoming the Church's top priority. The urgency of reaching children for Christ before age 13 has resulted in an abundance of ministry ideas and opportunities. It's an exciting time for children's pastors and teachers and they are busier than ever!

That's why Gospel Light's *Smart Pages* are the perfect resource for people involved in children's ministry. They help leaders evaluate the purpose and goals of their programming, and then help them develop the practical elements for realizing their ministry goals. Tested by teachers and leaders, the information in these comprehensive resources has been proven to work in real-life children's ministries.

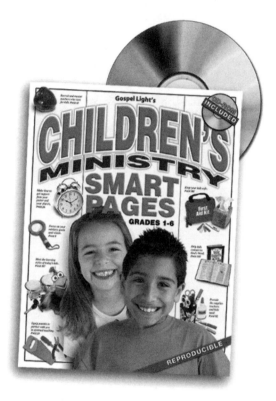

Preteen Ministry Smart Pages

Gordon and Becki West

Gordon and Becki West offer a solid, practical and comprehensive understanding of how to build an effective ministry that reaches this vital age group. Covers such topics as understanding preteens, making preteen youth groups work, motivating and nurturing preteens, ministering to the families of preteens, and recruiting and managing ministry volunteers.

Anyone who has a heart for helping kids make the difficult transition from childhood to adolescence will find a wealth of information and ideas in this rich and much-needed resource.

ISBN 08307.37111

Children's Ministry Smart Pages with CD-ROM

This comprehensive guide provides you with all the information you need to create an effective children's ministry. Reproducible.

This book also includes—
• Miniposters that highlight key teaching skills
• A CD-ROM containing everything that's in the book

ISBN 08307.30966

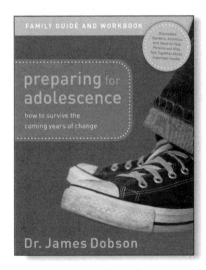